Design & Decorate

Interiors

Design & Decorate

Interiors

Lesley Taylor

NEW
HOLLAND

CONTENTS

INTRODUCTION • page 6

Layout and planning • page 8

Colour scheming • page 12

STYLE FILE • page 26

Traditional style • page 28

Contemporary style • page 48

Country and cottage style • page 68

Tranquil style • page 86

Children's rooms • page 102

Conservatory and garden rooms • page 116

Cloakrooms and shower rooms • page 122

Hallways • page 128

Studio rooms and bedsits • page 134

FOCUS FILE • page 142

Walls and floors • page 144

Window treatments • page 152

Fabrics and soft furnishings • page 158

Lighting • page 170

Storage solutions • page 176

Stockists • page 190

Index • page 191

INTRODUCTION

Designing and decorating the interior of your home should give many hours of pleasure, both in the creation and the enjoyment afterwards. But deciding on what style suits you best and how you should set about recreating it can pose some very difficult choices and this is where *Design and Decorate Interiors* comes into play.

Armed with this book you can first learn how to work out your needs and make the best use of your space in practical terms. There is a useful section devoted to that vital aspect of interior design – colour – and how it works. Of course, it is difficult to plan exactly what you require if you are still undecided as to your preferences for the finished decor. The core of the book is given over to helping you, as the Style File on pages 26-141 takes a close look at different kinds of decoration. Ranging from contemporary to country, and traditional to tranquil, each section looks in depth at a selection of rooms decorated in these varying styles. Sections dedicated to children's rooms, conservatories, cloakrooms, hallways and bedsits are also included. The text discusses the main decorative features and, more importantly, how you can achieve the same look in your own home.

The Focus File on pages 142-187 elaborates on the more practical elements of decorating each room. It concentrates on upholstery and soft furnishings, storage, walls and floor coverings, window treatments and lighting. Each aspect of the Focus File is written with the home decorator in mind, giving essential and realistic advice so that you can create a truly stylish home.

Layout and planning

To achieve the look you want, the layout of each room should be planned carefully. Be as imaginative as you like in your choice of decoration and furnishings. For example, if you are planning a new living room, two sofas, or a sofa and sofa bed, and/or several different, comfortable chairs are much more attractive to look at than the conventional three-piece suite. They are also easier to arrange and clever coordination can be achieved with the choice of covers. A sideboard or other storage/serving surface could be positioned back-to-back with the sofa, facing towards the dining end of the room, for easy access to the dining table. Don't forget to allow space for opening doors/drawers, or pushing back dining chairs from the table.

The symmetrical arrangement of the furniture and accessories in the entrance to this bay window creates a formal look – perfect for such a traditional setting.

When you are planning the layout for a bedroom, don't forget to allow for room doors and those on wardrobes opening into the room, and the distance that drawers pull out. Ample floor space should also be allocated around the bed.

When considering either a new or a renovated bathroom, there are various factors to take into account: the siting of the exterior plumbing, the range of fixtures (bath and/or shower, toilet, washbasin, bidet) and their style, whether contemporary or classic, fitted or free-standing. Before narrowing down the choices, however, it's important to make a floor plan of your bathroom to check that everything will fit. It is simplest to do this on graph paper and to a scale of say 1 to 20, this means that 1 cm (1 in) on the

Traditional rooms with fireplaces often have alcoves on each side – the ideal position for fitted wardrobes, and an excellent use of what could be wasted space.

graph paper will represent 20 cm (20 in) of the actual room. Mark the walls, doors and windows as well as the site of the soil pipe and any other existing plumbing, such as radiators. Next make scaled down versions of the fixtures on separate pieces of graph paper – all manufacturers' brochures will give size details – and move them around on the floor plan until you are satisfied with the layout.

There are many space-saving fixtures and fittings for bathrooms, to enable you to make the most of what is often one of the smallest rooms in the house. Showers can be fitted into baths, for example; baths and basins can be corner-fitted.

When it comes to kitchens, planning the layout can be quite complicated, as you have to take into account safety aspects as well as a design that is both practical and attractive. You may prefer to leave it to an expert in kitchen design. Kitchen designers will visit your home to discuss your requirements, gaining enough information to produce a plan and layout that they feel will best meet your individual needs from within their range of products. Don't be afraid to shop around, and if you find a style of kitchen

Making a plan of your bathroom will give you an overhead view, as here, of the fixtures and the space between them.

Narrow galley kitchens need careful planning to maximise the space. Here is a tried and tested layout with ample work surfaces and all the facilities close to hand.

from one company that particularly appeals to you, but prefer the ideas on layout suggested by another, feel free to discuss these alternatives with the designer.

For every room you intend to decorate, once a suitable plan has been decided, draw the items onto the floor plan. Leave these plans for a day or two before starting work; you can then take a fresh look to see that no mistakes have been made. Now is also a good time to check that there are sufficient electrical sockets for your requirements and that light fittings are in the relevant positions for your chosen layout.

Colour scheming

The same space can be given very different looks with skilful use of colour. Shades of blue maximize space; red creates warmth and intimacy; acid yellow adds life and vibrancy; clean, crisp greens and blues create a fresh look; contrasting blue and pink make perfect companions; cool blue meets restful green, creating calm.

Colour is undoubtedly the most important tool available to anyone decorating their home as it can add life and vitality to an uninspiring room. It also has the power to produce a variety of moods and an atmosphere that can affect the very quality of life lived by its occupants. You can use colour to make a small room look larger and more spacious, or to make a large room smaller and more intimate. By the subtle use of colour alone you can warm up a north-facing room or cool down the sunniest of walls.

We live in a colourful world, so why are so many of us hesitant when it comes to applying colour in our own homes? Possibly it is because we have only recently entered an age where technological advances enable us to produce paints, fabrics and wall coverings in practically any desired shade. This is such a contrast to the old safe approach to decorating chosen by our parents, that I am sure we merely require time to adjust.

Colour requires both confidence and caution. It is the easiest, cheapest way to transform a room — and the most daring. Which is why, if we are to use it successfully, we must learn how colour works, harness its

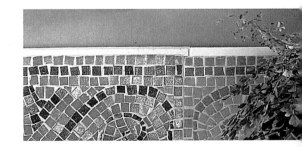

powers and use it in an educated manner. Once you understand colour, you then have the ability to transform your surroundings, creating an atmosphere unique to you.

The colour wheel

Colour is so powerful that it can transform the quality of a room in terms of mood and proportion, so a knowledge of colour theory is invaluable to the home decorator and designer. By understanding the colour wheel, for example, choosing an accent to pep up a bland room becomes a far simpler exercise.

The wheel is broken up into three basic colour types: primary, secondary, and tertiary (or intermediate) colours. Primary colours are the only ones that cannot be made by the mixing of other colours and these create the foundation of all theory. They are red, yellow and blue (at 11 o'clock, 3 o'clock and 7 o'clock on the photograph opposite).

Secondary colours are derived from mixing together equal amounts of two primary colours. For example, yellow mixed with red will give you orange (1 o'clock, opposite), blue and yellow creates green (5 o'clock), and blue and red produces violet (9 o'clock). These are known as the secondary colours. Tertiary or intermediate colours fall between the secondary hues and supply us with many different shades.

Now that you are familiar with the colour wheel you can begin to understand some of the other categories. Harmonious colours all have the same base, for example, blue, as in green-blue, violet-blue and violet. They are found next to each other on the colour wheel. These colours always combine well and when used together create a scheme that is easy on the eye.

Contrasting colours are those that lie opposite each other on the wheel, the strongest of which are direct opposites, such as

The colours in the colour wheel are always found in the same position because each colour, whether it is secondary, intermediate, or a shade in between, is always achieved by mixing the same proportions of the original colours.

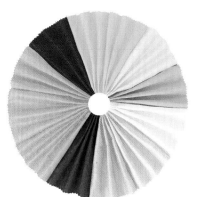

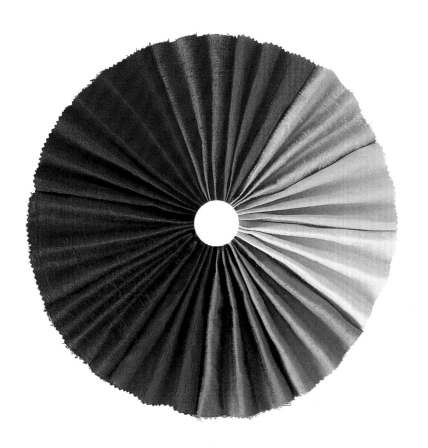

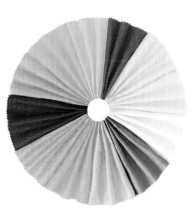

*SECONDARY
COLOURS*

green and orange or lavender and yellow. If you are decorating a room with two contrasting colours, be cautious, and always make sure that one dominates or you could have a scheme that is difficult to live with, as they tend to compete.

The colours in the wheel can also fall into two further categories: warm and cool. Warm colours are found on the top of the wheel; choose these if you want a cosy and welcoming colour scheme. Warm colours draw in a room and they include reds, yellows, pinks and oranges. Cool colours, however, tend to have a calming effect on a room, making it look more spacious and formal. These colours are found on the opposite side of the wheel and include violets, and shades of blues and greens.

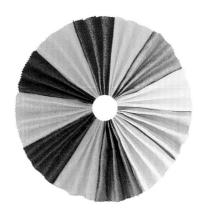

*TERTIARY
COLOURS*

The power of colour

Choosing colours for a room gives a wonderful opportunity to make a powerful statement. In the imaginatively planned bathroom shown here, three bold paint colours with matching tiles, cleverly combining two warm with one cool shade, are used to delineate the different areas, producing a vibrant, lively effect.

When choosing the colours for your kitchen, don't forget that it is one of the first rooms in which you spend time each morning so the colours used should look as good in daylight as in the evening when you entertain. Also remember that colour is supplied by china, utensils and, sometimes, glassware. These will

Primary colours matched with white sanitary ware accentuate the different levels, fittings and recesses of this modern bathroom. Glass shelves provide a neutral base for matching towels and toiletries.

have a great impact upon the colour balance of a room.

The same rules apply when you are planning the colour scheme for a bedroom. Here, too, colours need to look as good in the evening as in the morning light. It is best to avoid very bright hues as they may prove disturbing if the room is used during a bout of illness. However, should you want a bolder colour scheme, the earthy and toning shades of terracotta, rich cream and black can offer an effective option.

To make the best of a medley of colours you need to get the lighting just right. In the absence of natural light, use pure white halogen lighting, adding interest with spots and concealed lights.

Understanding tone

Whileile colour is very powerful and adds atmosphere to a room, it is the way in which we use tone that affects the actual shape of the finished room.

The word tone describes the lightness or darkness of a colour, and this is altered by the addition of black or white. I find the easiest way to translate colour into tone is to imagine the room or item you are considering as it would be seen in a black and white photograph. If it was all of the same tonal value, the picture would appear completely flat. It is only the variation of tone that adds depth to the photograph. As a general guide, dark colours advance

This well-planned, neutral scheme shows just how important tone is when planning a colour scheme.

These drawings show how tone can be used to improve the proportions of a room or disguise problem areas.

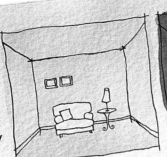

To make a room feel larger, decorate in light colours as light is then reflected.

To bring the walls in and ceiling down, use warm colours.

Dark and warm colours advance. A wall painted in a dark colour is drawn in.

Cool colours recede. A wall painted in a cool colour appears further away.

A dark floor covering makes the floor seem smaller and draws the eye downwards.

To lower a ceiling use a colour which is slightly darker than the walls.

To raise a ceiling use a colour which is lighter than the walls.

To lower a ceiling in a large room paint the top section of the walls to match.

To widen a corridor use a very light colour on the walls, ceiling and floor.

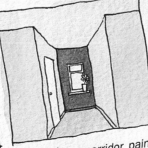

To shorten a corridor, paint the end wall in a dark or warm colour.

To alter the proportions of a corridor, decorate the ceiling and floor in a darker colour.

while pale colours recede as they reflect more light, making a room appear larger. This is why so many modern properties have their rooms, and ceilings in particular, painted white: in order to create the illusion of space and height.

Tone can be used to great effect in a narrow hallway or corridor. By applying a darker tone to the ceiling than the walls (and in some case on properties with very tall ceilings, by bringing the same tone down to the picture rail), you considerably reduce the appearance of the ceiling height. By adding a floor covering which is also of a deeper tone than the walls, you can create the effect of pushing back the walls, making the corridor appear very much wider.

Another common problem in modern properties is the long sitting room with its windows at one or either end on the narrow walls. By applying the theory of dark colours advancing, a substantial pair of curtains in a tone deeper than the walls can successfully draw in the window walls. In this way, the proportions of the room are visually adjusted, making it appear squarer (see the illustration on page 19 for other ways to improve on the proportions of your rooms).

Many people enjoy the calm simplicity of a monochromatic colour scheme: a room decorated only in tones of one colour. The room opposite, for example, is decorated in a variety of blues such as lavender blue and green blue. But, in addition, there are varying strengths of tone included, creating a finished scheme of great visual interest.

Imagine this room with the door coloured the same tone as the walls, and with the white woodwork and picture frame painted in a green blue. If this were the case, the room would have much less impact and would look very flat and rather uninteresting.

The calm simplicity of this scheme comes from the consideration of cool colour and varying tones. By using different shades of blue, greater interest is given to the room.

Accents and contrasts

Have you ever experienced that disheartening feeling when you have spent weeks planning your new room? You have deliberated, pondered and agonized over the patterns, shades and the important tones of your room, only to stand back and view your finished room in the knowledge that 'there is something definitely missing'. Well, the possibility is that if the room has been well planned and is made up of one or two well-balanced colours it will benefit from the use of an accent colour – a different, contrasting colour – to give relief and dimension to your room.

Accents don't have to come in the form of a fabric, paint or wall covering. In fact, these would quite often offer too large a block of colour. Instead, the occasional lamp, picture or even well-placed blanket or throw can be the perfect solution.

Accents should always be used with restraint, less is more is definitely the right approach. Use them in patches and don't dot them around. If you use a tonal variation of the colour that predominates in your colour scheme, it will no longer act as an accent. Instead, it will become part of the main colour scheme, making the room too busy. One carefully chosen cushion in your accent colour will have more of an impact on your room than four of the same all positioned like soldiers on your sofa.

The bedroom featured here is the perfect example of a well-used accent. The room is made up of equal portions of the blue and cream checked fabric and the plain wall panelling. The colours are soft, and while there is an interesting mix of plaid and check, the red accent is needed to pep up the scheme. The red in this case is a contrast accent because it is a colour found on the opposite side of the colour wheel to the blue of the main scheme. A number of other accent colours could have been used in this room, such as pink and pale yellow, but the red offers the most impact, precisely because it is such a contrast.

The red picture and blankets act as a very successful accent in this room, contrasting with the predominant blue of the check bedding and curtains.

An uncluttered hallway painted in bright yellow and white is given a contrasting accent with the addition of a striking black vase.

Contrast accents are perfect for adding definition to a mono-chromatic scheme where shades and tones are all of one colour. A room decorated in different shades of peach, for example, will always look good with the addition of a green accent (again, shades that are not close together on the colour wheel). This could be in the form of plants grouped in the corner of the room together with, perhaps, a small green footstool placed on the opposite side for balance.

Likewise, a soft blue (a cool colour) bedroom can benefit from the warmth introduced by a small touch of pink, such as a bowl of flowers, or a soft pink blanket folded at the foot of the bed.

As you become familiar with the effects of a coloured accent on a room you will soon begin to recognize examples of this technique when you look through your favourite interiors magazines. You will also notice rooms that would benefit from the addition of an accent here and there. But be tactful, not everyone will take kindly to you offering them the benefit of your newly found knowledge.

This yellow nursery, furnished principally in white, is offset by a few accents of blue. Imagine the room without the accent; it would be rather uninteresting.

STYLE FILE

By now you will be familiar with the way colour and tone can affect a room, and I am confident that you can handle accents and monochromatic schemes with ease. These are all the basis of good design practice, but to be able to turn your hand to confident interior design you need to be familiar with the various styles of decor.

The style of curtain you choose, and the shape and colour of your sofa all have an effect on the look of your finished room. A feather-filled chintz sofa would look completely out of place in a Mediterranean-style living room, for example. In the same way, a hand-painted terracotta pot would have no place sitting in a Georgian garden room. Learning what styles of furniture and furnishings work together to create a certain look is very important and one of the simplest ways of doing this is by flipping through a range of interiors magazines. By breaking down the rooms into elements such as style of curtains, fabrics used, design of wallpapers, and the finish of the fireplaces, you will soon find that you identify the items that set the style of the room, those that enhance it and those that you would not choose to incorporate yourself.

In Style File, we feature each of the rooms in the house decorated in different colourways and styles, and then discuss how the colours and elements are best put together to create a wide range of looks.

Loft spaces are frequently very bright and airy with a large proportion of wall space given over to windows. In this room, maximum play is made of the light by painting the walls and ceiling white. The dark blue in the furnishings and carpet successfully keeps the living area "grounded".

TOP LEFT

The traditional Georgian red is given a contemporary twist with the sponged panels and hand-painted fish.

TOP RIGHT

Muted colours, a plaid fabric and wood combine in an easy simplicity. The ties on the bedding add to this home-spun feel.

BOTTOM LEFT

Cornflower blue and soft green contrast with sunshine yellow, pink and orange in this surprisingly coordinated sitting room.

BOTTOM RIGHT

The old and the new are unified by timeless yellow paint on the walls and traditional fabric over the chair seats.

Traditional style

Traditional rooms are those that include an element or theme derived from the past. This does not mean, however, that they have to be decorated in a pure form of a particular period. Elements of Georgian styling can successfully be mixed with turn-of-the-century pieces to give the room an individual, yet still traditional feel.

Here, the walls have been split using a dado rail which helps to lower the high ceiling and creates a Victorian atmosphere. The proportions of the room are such that it could appear rather grand, and while a swag pelmet has been chosen, it is in an informal style using a soft fabric. The under curtain made from a fine sheer fabric diffuses and softens the light which could otherwise be a little harsh through such a large window. The wooden floor which has been stripped and varnished, brings an old-fashioned quality to the room, enhancing the traditional feel.

A pair of lamps have been positioned on either side of the fireplace, highlighting the recesses when illuminated. This switches the focal point of the room from the window in the daytime towards the chimney breast in the evening.

The carefully grouped pictures above the sofa enable the owner of the house to bring some of his or her personality into the room.

This well-proportioned room has been decorated to produce a fresh and comfortable – yet traditional – living space. The pale shades of green and yellow are cool and relaxing.

Green is a secondary colour derived from yellow (mixed with blue) and therefore they work in harmony with each other.

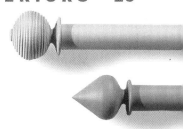

They have been arranged so that none of the pictures is above the height of the traditional-style overmantel mirror. In this way the height of the room is visually lowered as the eye-line is kept to a comfortable level.

Don't forget the details. Accessories, such as curtain poles, can be bought or painted to colour coordinate with your chosen scheme.

Pattern creates an old-fashioned feel

Personalize your living room with old boxes that are treated with an antiquing paint effect and then covered with decoupage.

The use of pattern in your interior decorating schemes is one way in which you can introduce elements of a traditional style into the different rooms of your home.

While you will want to choose patterns that reflect the era you wish to recreate, it is also important to choose a pattern which suits the size and shape of the surface on which it is to be used. Employ bold designs on large areas and discreet patterns on smaller surfaces. Also, plan the position of the pattern carefully so that you don't get any awkward cut-off points (tops of trees or flowers, or animal heads missing at the tops of walls or curtains). Ensure that the main motifs are correctly centred, say above the backs of sofas and fireplaces. Take care with the strength of colour too. Pale and mid-tones work best on smaller surfaces, whereas bolder ones can be used on large walls and floors, or at important windows.

In this warm, old-fashioned living room, pattern has been used cleverly to create an impression of greater height — vertical stripes help to 'raise' the ceiling. The ceiling is painted the same colour as the paler, soft rose background of the stripe — another visual trick to increase the height. Contrary to popular belief, white ceilings do not necessarily look higher, unless they are combined with white walls, or where the background to a wall covering is white.

The pattern mix has been cleverly coordinated. The striped drapes are slightly different to the

This decor relies on a rich combination of colour and pattern. Mix terracotta, forest green or royal blue stripe wallcoverings with William Morris-style printed fabrics and add architectural mouldings if your room lacks these vital period elements.

wallpaper, but from the same colour palette, so they blend well with the walls and yet define the window recess. The checked and striped upholstery on the armchair and chaise longue act as a neutral link between wall and window treatments, the sofa and the formal geometric motifs on the floor.

The lighting is mainly provided by decorative lamps, in keeping with the traditional style of the room. In addition, there is lighting on the ceiling and on the tables to enhance certain accessories.

Texture has been considered carefully in this living room, with gilt frames, touches of alabaster and brass, and polished woods all contrasting with the matt walls, silky-striped chaise and a "nubbly" needlepoint rug.

Modern paints revive an old kitchen

A few years ago, kitchen designers looked for inspiration to the traditional cook's kitchen found in the servants' quarters of large, old houses. This led to a revival of the painted wooden kitchen. The old kitchens were very well designed with ample storage, and incorporated whole walls of cupboards and drawers. The up-to-date version of this area offers the home a well-organized space with a traditional air. The cream paintwork associated with this style of kitchen is still very popular, but has also given way to a more contemporary range of colours, giving the basic design a modern feel.

The kitchen featured here is the perfect example of a new style of cook's kitchen where modern paints are mixed with traditional pieces of furniture to create a warm and welcoming family space. The beauty of this sort of kitchen is its ability to work well in so many different types of house. It looks equally at home in a small, surburban house as it does in a large old country manor.

Appliances such as dishwashers are housed in matching units to help retain the character of this kind of kitchen. While most styles of hob and oven would work successfully in this setting, traditional ranges, such as the one featured opposite, fully enhance the design features that were originally part of this type of kitchen.

This particular colour scheme uses light yellow painted walls

Ceramic tiles have a rich and interesting history. Originating in Persia and China, it was many hundreds of years before glazed tiles were discovered in Europe. Today, many manufacturers and some individual potteries offer handmade tiles fashioned by traditional methods.

as a summery backdrop behind the peppermint green units and painted furniture. Schemes featuring traditional wallpapers or stencilling would be equally successful. If you choose this option, ensure the wallpapers used are vinyl coated to withstand the moisture created by cooking. Likewise, use paints that are specifically designed for steamy kitchen use. These are usually water based and incredibly easy to apply. The tiled walls behind the work surfaces and cooking area are a practical – as well as decorative – finishing touch as they are quick to put up and easy to wipe down.

Painted kitchens always offer the option of re-styling, as you can simply change the colour in years to come. This means you can give your room a new lease of life without installing a new kitchen. Simply sand back the original woodwork to enable the new paint to key, and apply at least two coats of suitable paint.

Mellow wood and rich colours for an aged look

Initially, it is the deep burgundy red that greets the eye in this room, but the blue vase and fruit bowl in the foreground go a long way towards alleviating what might otherwise be an unremitting heaviness.

The units in this characterful kitchen are a basic dark oak, but it is the bold decoration that gives the room its atmosphere. The dark crimson balances well with the wood, and while it could have appeared quite heavy, the decorator has chosen a gloss finish for the painted walls, taking advantage of its reflective qualities. Both windows are undressed to allow for maximum light, and the ledges on the lower sash windows supply an

additional display area for the owner's beloved collection of china dogs.

A paper border brings relief from the plain walls and introduces pattern to the room. This links with the fabric on the carved oak chair, while a larger scale pattern on the kelim rug decorates the floor. An old plate rack adds extra storage and, grouped together with old wooden trays, it supplies a further interesting feature.

It is not only the colour of a ceramic bowl that enhances a colour scheme, but the fruit that is in it, too. A judicious choice of contents can bring a strong accent to your kitchen.

This kitchen is very homely and looks as if it has evolved over the years. The secret to this form of decorating is to keep to historical colours, use a blend of older wooden chairs and cupboards, and display your favourite collection of china and books. Historical colours are often used by designers to create archive-style fabrics and wall coverings. There is currently a revival in historical type paints, such as distemper and casein, and many manufacturers are now producing collections that include traditional colours from various times in history such as Georgian and Victorian. These are perfect for use in traditionally decorated rooms such as this kitchen.

The electrical points in this room have been painted to blend with the walls (blocks of white in a colour scheme like this would look very obvious indeed). As an alternative to painting points, it is also possible to buy coloured or even transparent ones.

Old wooden pieces of furniture and carved animals add a rustic charm to the traditional room.

Italian renaissance revival profiles strong colour

This traditional dining room is the perfect location for a formal dinner party. The terracotta red walls offer warmth during the day, but take on a far softer appearance in the evening. This colour works particularly well in candlelight, and as the dining room is the one room in the house that you are most likely to light in this manner, it is the perfect colour (together with darker and lighter tones) to use here.

The fully upholstered dining chairs are covered in sky blue damask that contrasts strongly with the terracotta walls. The chairs have been finished off with a rope detail at the back – don't forget that the backs of dining chairs are usually seen more than the front. Although the wall panelling below the dado rail enhances the formal air of this room, the lack of heavily dressed curtains adds a simplicity to it that ensures the overall effect is not too grand.

The room is lit by a large central pendant in a rococo style which is very masculine in appearance with strong lines. A dining room lit by one central light will always benefit from having a dimmer switch fitted so that the levels of lighting can be varied very simply to alter the atmosphere within the room.

There is nothing nicer than a fully dressed dining table. The china and table dressings have just as

Choose your cutlery and china to enhance the colours of your finished room. Here the deep red is the perfect match for the painted walls.

Damask fabric and rich historical colours have been combined with carefully chosen accessories to create this elegant and stylish dining room.

much of an impact on the finished look of your room as do the upholstery and curtaining. Choose cutlery and china that are sympathetic to the decor of your room, not only in terms of colour but also in shape and pattern; they should all enhance your chosen theme.

Contrasting colours, just a few tones removed from their primary shades of red and blue, can be used to great effect.

French-style elegance creates a continental air

Less is more has always been my approach to home decorating, and here a careful blend of antique furniture and simple furnishings is the perfect example of such a philosophy. Keeping things simple does not mean that the end result need be bland or uninteresting. In fact, a well-chosen period object carefully positioned can have more of an impact on a room than a whole collection of antiques.

The warm, yet neutral, shades used on the walls and floor create the perfect backdrop to the rich antique coffer and linen press. The gilded cane bedhead adds a French air to the room and works particularly well in a room of this proportion (a dark mahogany headboard would have made it look heavier and more crowded).

Simple cream curtaining softens the hard edges of the sash windows while also adding to the lightness of the colour scheme. Note how the crisp white bed linen and cream curtaining give the light walls a richer colour. This is a good trick to remember as, in rooms with little sunlight or those that are on the small side, it is good to be able to achieve a richness but without making the room heavy and dark.

While the majority of this colour scheme is in neutral tones, a cream and

When considering a colour scheme, the upholstery on a chair is as important as the chair itself, as both need to fit comfortably into the finished room. If you upholster a chair in a fabric that is tonally similar to the finish on the wood, as here, the addition of a contrasting cushion will normally add life and depth to its appearance. But, as you can see here, it does not necessarily have to be a striking contrast.

opaline toile de Jouy fabric has been selectively used as a bed valance, a practical Roman blind and to upholster the two Regency, brass-mounted chairs at the foot of the bed. This fabric adds delicate detail without detracting from the room's uncluttered appearance.

As with all well-decorated rooms, accessories play an important part. The floor-length gilt mirror in the far corner of the room opens out what could have been a dull, dark space. The plants and flowers add life and additional colour, and they tie in beautifully with the botanical prints above the bed.

Creams, buttermilks and whites work beautifully together. However, to create a successful scheme you need contrast of tone – here provided by the dark wooden furniture – to add punctuation to the room. Imagine this room with pale wooden or painted furniture – the overall effect would lack depth and richness.

Classic decor in white and cream

Colour can have such a pronounced effect on your mood that careful consideration should always be taken when choosing it for your home. Nowhere is this more important than in the bedroom which, for most people, is a sanctuary from everyday life.

This room has used a combination of clever decorating tricks: the warm gold used here is one of the most comforting in the spectrum; the stripes in the wallpaper add height to the room, while the plain cream curtains and bed drapes with their beautifully scrunched headings add softness. (To achieve this, make the curtains very full — at least three times the width of the space — and sew very deep casings. Stuff the casings with spare fabric for a puffy effect.)

The fabric is a clever device as stripes can often add a harsh formality to a room. Patterned glazed cotton introduced on the headboard and scatter cushions draw attention to the bed and bring together all the main colours in the room.

The bed has been dressed in white bed linen; many people would not consider using white in a scheme with so much cream, but it actually adds a crispness, and white used directly next to cream always creates a richer look. A deep green has been selected for the bed valance, this colour echoed on the headboard.

Lighting is very important in a bedroom, not only for practical use but for highlighting items, such as an ornate bed dressing, or a dressing table, adding a further dimension to the scheme and

Select an ornate style of lamp for a bedroom such as this to follow through the classical theme.

attracting attention to different areas of the room.

Finally, attention to detail is important: the classic bedside lamps, the picture hung from oversized tassels over the bed, and the fabric rose on the tieback all provide visual interest.

A puffed curtain heading above the bed and as a matching window treatment is easy to create yet provides a chic and eye-catching finish.

Fully furnished recreates the look of a century past

Above: The flower-shaped basin complements the period wallpaper.
Below: Deep colours and an old-fashioned suite imbue the bathroom with Victorian charm.

A larger room, perhaps converted from a surplus bedroom, offers the ideal opportunity to choose original or reproduction period bathroom furniture and accessorize it with ornaments, plants, rugs, and prints — even adding a sofa or chaise longue.

This Victorian- and Edwardian-style sanitary ware is snowy-white and curvaceous. Ornately decorated with wrought iron brackets, enamelled flowers and butterflies, it is teamed with warm mahogany which provides a rich, glossy effect.

Here are all the classic features: the roll-top, free-standing bath; the generously lipped basin; the decorated toilet with its high-level, cast-metal cistern. The colour scheme is strictly

traditional too: glowing terracotta for the floor tiles and strong, bottle-green on the walls to dado level, enlivened with a typical tiled wide border and ribbed edgings.

In rooms like these, it is the bath that must enjoy centre stage: use paint to colour it, stencil or marble it, and raise it up in the middle of the room on sturdy ball and claw feet, lion's paws or gilded shells. In the main picture (opposite) the bath has been set at a slight angle for extra interest. Alternatively, the roll-top can be elegantly panelled in against a wall with polished or painted tongue-and-groove timber to match other furnishings and fittings.

But it is the carefully chosen accessories and decorative touches that reinforce the correct period atmosphere. Design features such as a striped wallpaper; heavy reproduction tiles; sturdy brass taps; stained glass at the window, and, if you have the space, a parlour palm, can transform even a modern plain white suite into a Victorian sanctuary.

Despite its air of opulence, the look is strong and dramatic, perfect for those seeking a more masculine style for the bathroom.

Red plush, gleaming brass and etched glass comfortably embrace the modern convenience of electric candle sconces and a power shower, without losing the period atmosphere.

Classical themes reinterpreted with modern materials

The colour scheme alone in this bold bathroom — ochre, black and russet — is enough to suggest you have stepped into a scene from an Etruscan vase, yet the classical angle has been developed still further with the witty use of furniture and accessories. Was it the set of monochromatic urn prints that suggested the theme; the elegant statuette; or the magnificent free-standing tub with its frieze, reminiscent of Roman marble baths?

The traditional saffron colour of the walls is sufficient to warm and soften the dominant black and white elements and, cleverly, the temptation to use ceramic tiles has been resisted, so avoiding any kind of cold, clinical atmosphere.

An oval mirror with an Italianate frame reflects the classical theme.

You no longer need be restrained by splashbacks and large tiled areas thanks to modern paints which can resist moisture and may

even be specially formulated for use on areas where there is a risk of water splashes or condensation. Even if you have set your heart on wallpaper in the bathroom, a couple of coats of non-yellowing varnish will offer protection to areas not directly in contact with water. And a sheet of clear perspex screwed to the wall over vulnerable areas should keep your design ideas compatible with the practical requirements of a bathroom.

In the bathroom illustrated, style has not been allowed to become compromised by the needs of comfort and practicality. Parquet and a patterned rug on the floor give the impression of mosaic without

offering a cold, slippery surface underfoot. The single tasselled

curtain on its iron pole is a popular modern window treatment; yet

also hints at spears and togas.

Accessorizing with unusual ornaments and possessions will

also help to personalize the overall look. Note how in this room,

an antique occasional table and tapestry-style rug give it a charac-

ter and comfort not usually associated with bathrooms.

The luxury of space has been handled carefully with restrained decoration and elegant fittings to produce a room that is both classical and comfortable.

Total white-out
keeps mind and body refreshed

The minimalist approach to design works extremely well in a room which is purely functional. Here, the scheme is white-on-white with an unexpected burst of orange, relying mainly on shapes and textures for variety and interest. There are no frills, no superfluous furnishings: the light from the naked window illuminates only the white stained boards and beams of floor and ceiling. In today's approach to uncluttered living, this is an excellent design to emulate.

Even the roughly plastered walls offer no distraction from the room's centrepiece: the modern interpretation of an old Victorian

An old-fashioned room has been given the full monastic treatment with an all-white scheme and a geometric modern suite to create a contemplative setting bathed in light.

roll-top bath with futuristic styling in warm-to-the-touch acrylic. Egg-cup bidet and toilet with an unusual cone-shaped basin complete this stunning suite.

It takes great single-mindedness to resist any temptation to use fabrics, floor coverings, pictures or ornaments of any kind; but here the absence of decoration allows the architecture of an old house to speak for itself. In a more modern room, without the character provided by the stripped boards, old beams and other period features, the overall effect would have been more clinical and less pleasing.

To achieve a similar effect in a bathroom where it hasn't been possible to hide all the pipes and wiring, simply prime and paint everything – wood, metal, cistern, outside of the bath, flooring – to match the walls and thus render them virtually invisible. Box-in awkward features first and consider incorporating cupboards to hide away all the essential but potentially untidy bathroom toiletries and cleaning materials.

For an even more effective disguise, use a flecked or textured paint over every surface. Variety can also be introduced into a monochrome scheme by using matt and gloss finishes, or stains and bleaches for timber instead of paint.

If you are fitting new sanitary ware, look for a suite with smooth lines and untextured surfaces. Sleek modern chrome mixer taps are a perfect and practical accompaniment.

Attention to detail is essential in a minimalist setting. These taps have the shape, style and class for any all-white and chrome bathroom scheme.

Contemporary style

Bright blocks of colour and straight runs of units make this kitchen truly contemporary.

Every few years there is a trend in interior design which, as with fashion, filters from the leading designers through to the high street. Over the last two decades we have seen a Victorian revival and the return of the country interior. But this has now made way for a new and refreshing trend that incorporates the bright and confident use of colour and clean, simple lines. It is the return of the streamlined and hi-tech contemporary interior.

The word "contemporary" is described in the dictionary as being of the same age or era, which simply means this style is current or of this period. So by its very nature, contemporary design includes a number of up-to-date styles, including the clean, modern look that is now so popular. Choosing to decorate your house in a contemporary way gives you a wide design spectrum to work within, along with the opportunity of being creative and individual in your approach.

If you are planning a contemporary kitchen, for example, you

One contemporary kitchen designer celebrates the style of the innovative and highly original Scottish designer and architect, Charles Rennie Mackintosh, with his interpretation of a "Mackintosh" kitchen.

may wish to choose blocks of bright, plain colours incorporated into highly glossed kitchen units, or modular wooden furniture teamed with chrome and modern plastics. Whatever you choose, this style enables you to use bold colour with confidence.

RIGHT: By using a monochromatic and plain colour scheme teamed with simple ornaments and furnishings, a traditional setting is given a modern look.

BELOW: Wonderful textures and splendid plant specimens combine to create a living room of immense variety and interest.

White and chrome
for an upbeat look

As with all colour schemes, the lighter the colours used, the larger the area in which they appear will look. Here, a fairly narrow kitchen leading to a dining area has benefited from the use of pure white units. Look at the area where the kitchen meets the dining room and imagine how tall and narrow the opening would have seemed if the units on either side had been a deeper colour.

White can have the disadvantage of giving a room a clinical and sometimes cold appearance, especially in north-facing rooms. This is because blocks of white can appear grey when natural light lacks the sun's warmth. One way to add softness to a white room is to opt for white or cream with a lemon base. There are, however, other ways of adding warmth to a basically white colour scheme. Using a warm colour like peach or terracotta in tiling, flooring or furnishings, for example, would soften the room, but beware, as a large expanse of white with a minimal amount of these colours can look contrived and quite uneasy on the eye.

One of the most successful ways of bringing a mellow warmth to a white room is to use natural timber, which has a way of softening the hard edges of a colour scheme. In this kitchen, the timber flooring, in particular, adds a casualness to a room that would have looked cold and unwelcoming if clad in more obvious white, grey or black ceramic or marble tiles.

The traditional toaster – with its enduring sense of style – has made a come-back and is the perfect design feature in a predominantly chrome kitchen.

The pattern in which the timber floor has been laid also has an effect on the appearance of the finished room. If the timber strips had been set to run the length of the kitchen through to the dining area, the floor would have looked longer, and the kitchen even narrower. If the strips had run horizontally, the room would have benefited from the appearance of extra width, but the lines of the kitchen might have appeared hard and square. The perfect solution was to run them diagonally, adding width and softer lines to the room.

This kitchen looks extremely smart with its chrome appliances and accessories. Chrome has long been used in commercial settings because of its practical and hygienic qualities, and these have now been harnessed by designers to add a functional feel to domestic kitchens.

Refreshing pastels
revamp a kitchen/diner

Most of us are now aware of the benefits of a kitchen/diner – a room in which to relax and entertain as well as to prepare and eat our meals. Some people will relocate their kitchen to a larger room in the home, such as a rarely used formal dining room. If this is not the answer for you, then a single-storey extension on an existing room, or a conservatory housing the working kitchen, may be the perfect solution. The pastel-painted kitchen featured here is an excellent example of a well-designed, compact and modern kitchen positioned in a single-storey extension to the side of a living space.

When planning a kitchen extension or refurbishment, it is a good idea to decide how much of your time will be spent preparing meals in the room, and how much time will be taken with activities more associated with a living or sitting room. If your kitchen is well designed, a great deal can be achieved in a very limited space: good planning is the key to a successful working kitchen (see pages 6-9). As much can be achieved by an organized cook in a small kitchen as in the most generous of spaces. You may therefore be surprised at how little space you need to allocate to the working kitchen. Really, all that is needed is adequate storage, a cooker, refrigerator, sink and sufficient preparation and serving spaces.

The attractive kitchen featured here benefits from the additional natural light supplied by the sky lights and further enhanced by the

It is the confident use of colour which lifts this kitchen from the mundane to the fabulous. The choice and balance of colours – pale mauve teamed with the palest creamy lemon and cobalt blue – can be carried from the overall decor through to the smaller details.

chosen colour scheme. Lemon-green wall and base units sit very happily on a lavender blue background. It is interesting to note that pastels are the only colours on the colour wheel that you can guarantee will never clash; it doesn't matter what combination you team together, they will always work successfully. The lavender blue walls and ceiling also act to maximize the available space as all blue-based, cool colours appear to recede, and therefore create the impression of pushing back the walls that they are being used to decorate.

Tonal interest is provided by the dark blue stained glass in the windows and the inset border on the tiled splashback. This important detail acts to emphasize the area, adding depth to a basically pastel colour scheme.

The island unit provides an additional work surface and lots of storage; it also acts as a natural divide between the working area of the kitchen and the dining or sitting room.

A sophisticated look on a budget

Coir matting is a tough floor covering that looks especially good in a neutral interior.

This perfectly styled, contemporary dining room is a great example of style on a budget. It is an achievable look for a first-time home owner or someone constantly moving house and wanting to keep furnishings to an absolute minimum.

The room is decorated using off-white emulsion paint, with the addition of one wall that has had a soft mushroom stripe applied, also with emulsion paint. This is a very cost-effective form of decorating; just use a plumb line or ruler and masking tape to achieve the stripes.

The carpet is a fine check in soft caramel and cream, as is the top tablecloth, and the change of scale between the two patterns means they do not compete. They are also broken up by the undercloth with its flowing calligraphy motif. By using floor-length tablecloths, you can employ any old table; it could even be an old metal patio table, or a tabletop made of chipboard.

Natural timber will always enhance a contemporary, neutral colour scheme as it is full of tone and texture.

Texture is as important as pattern in a room like this, and this design supplies lots of it in a very complementary way. The softness of the carpet, the coldness of smooth wrought iron, the rustic aged timber, cane basket work and the distressed terracotta work together very

well. You will find that textures derived from nature always work successfully in this type of scheme.

As this is a neutrally coloured room, it relies on changes of tone to be successful. Look at it as if it were a black and white photograph and you will see ample variation. The scheme is lifted by the introduction of a colour accent in the form of two green plants. Another advantage to this colour scheme is that it looks just as effective in the evening, with its soft candlelight from thc chandclier hanging above the table.

Texture is as important as pattern in a neutral colour scheme. The carpet featured above could have been replaced with the natural coir matting shown opposite for a slightly different effect.

Blend bright primary shades for colourful chic

A deep yellow wall has been bravely anchored by dramatic midnight blue and white to give a nautical flavour to this bright bathroom.

Bold primary colours needn't be overwhelming if you choose your shades carefully. Limiting yourself to a mainly two-colour scheme helps keep the look chic and modern, away from nursery-style, multi-colour combinations.

This upbeat, yet coolly smart, bathroom seems to have taken its theme from

the beach with its deep sea-blues and soft sand yellow, highlighted by touches of bright white and chrome. Another reason why it works so well is the sleek modern styling of the sanitary ware, even the plumbing and lighting are designed to be invisible.

Although shiny surfaces predominate, there is variety in the all-over satin sheen of the floor, the smoky effect of the opaque glass, the rough-brushed finish of the painted wall, and the multi-faceted surfaces of the mosaic tiles. The pleasantly rounded profiles of the basin, bidet and toilet are balanced by geometric squares of differing sizes, from the yellow wall of "tiles" behind the basin, to the tiny mosaics in blues and greens.

When using strong colours, a dramatic, yet simple approach like this one will put them into context and prevent them looking out of place. You need new and clever ideas, unusual accessories, or

This free-standing shelf and towel rail unit is highly practical but also provides a display area for colours and objects to complement the general room scheme.

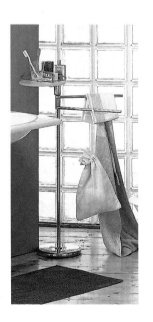

special decorative effects to complement the loud statement you are making in colour.

Here, confident use of colour has also been used successfully to draw attention away from an awkwardly shaped room. The continuous coverage of the blue across floor and wall gives the room unity and focuses attention on the yellow area.

Seaside colours are crisp and inviting in this sleek, yellow and blue bathroom.

Explore the freshness of lemon and lime

A small second bathroom destined for use by guests or children, is the perfect opportunity to have fun and give your imagination full rein. Light is often limited to a small window or skylight, so keep the decoration bright but rather than opting for an all-over white, which can look too harsh and chilly, especially if the room is north-facing, choose a more subtle blend of creams,

Bright and cheerful, this room relies for its impact on a burst of colour against more neutral tones.

fresh lime and lemon pastels. Cheerful splashes of stronger colour can be used to add impact without being overpowering.

Cream tiles give a softer overall appearance than bright white.

This compact room has an airy, almost spacious feel to it thanks to mint-fresh green and near-neutral blue grid wallpapers, that cleverly disguise a high window and awkward shape. The whole scheme is linked by a single curtain and wide frieze that add just the right amount of sunny yellow and forget-me-not blue to produce a youthful vitality.

Maintaining that young, vibrant atmosphere, other elements are equally well chosen. The bath is panelled and the seat is wooden, but in a subtle ash effect to provide warmth and texture without any depth of colour. Similarly, the floor is varnished wood — but in cool blonde tones. In contrast, the fittings are shiny chrome to match that other essential bathroom accessory given an unusual modern twist in the designer mirror made of beaten metal plates. Potted plants and cut flowers maintain the freshness of appeal of this scheme and are a welcoming touch in a guest bathroom.

Keeping the same basic elements, it would be quick and inexpensive to give this room a totally new look, should you feel like a change. Replace the curtain with a painted, slatted blind and cover the frieze with matching dado rail to convert it to sleek minimalism. Alternatively, if the room was later intended for children, a picture roller blind at the window and a colourful nursery border would be great fun.

Yellow and blue is always a fresh, lively combination and its popularity ensures that matching vases, toothbrushes, towels, etc, are easy to find.

Minimalist furnishings for a modern bedroom

As there are currently so many contemporary design trends upon which to draw, it gives a very broad spectrum indeed for planning a bedroom. Two of the most obvious styles for a contemporary bedroom that most readily spring to mind are rooms furnished in a minimalist manner, and those decorated with neutral colours and natural furnishings.

Shades of beige and cream accompanied by seagrass matting with textured cottons and linens sit very comfortably together to create a neutral look. A minimalist impression can be created with a few well-chosen pieces. Remember, though, that this look may turn out to be quite expensive as each individual item has to make a "statement".

Modern lines are clean and hard-edged. A graphic bedstead in gun metal steel forms the nucleus of the bedroom decor. Keep colours bold and striking or neutral and understated. Select a stylized standard lamp for an unusual bedside light.

One of the most pleasing things about this type of styling is that it does not have to follow an historical or period style. The purist approach to decor need not be pursued and if you have furniture from a mixture of eras and in a range of styles, there is every possibility that you can find a suitable way of uniting them.

The other element that is becoming increasingly used in the contemporary interior is the influence of other cultures. Adopt the ideas wholesale or adapt them to fit in with your environment. In all, contemporary style gives enormous freedom and can afford you the opportunity of being creative.

ABOVE: Modern colours and check fabrics give this room its contemporary feel. Combining green and blue might not immediately strike you as being a great idea. However, as you can see, they work together surprisingly well. Tester pots of paint are invaluable for experimenting.

LEFT: Natural or neutral colour schemes consist of a blend of creams through to brown, plus the non-colours white and black. A successful room will have a variety of textures and tones, adding interest and depth to the room.

Tribal culture influences new designs

Traditional wood-carvings make beautiful additions to any room, especially in a bedroom with a tribal theme.

Tribal design has been popular for quite a time, illustrating as it does the rich history, cultures and philosophies of many different ethnic groups. The room shown opposite, for example, has a rustic charm, with a simple beamed ceiling and a ceramic floor which works particularly well with the chosen fabrics. In fact, the room and its elements look as if they truly belong together. The colours used in the tribal designs originate from natural dyes and colour pigments and it is the continuity of these colours into the main colour scheme that is the secret to the room's decorative success.

As the bedding makes such a design statement, pattern elsewhere in the room has been kept to a minimum, with accessories providing the detail. Especially noticeable, of course, are the paintings which have been chosen for their appropriate colours rather than subject matter. The one exception is the tribal mask, currently residing on the bed, which serves to remind us of the starting point for this decorative theme. The positioning of the rich wooden furniture adds balance to the room. If, for example, the far wall did not have the mahogany chest of drawers, the foreground would outweigh the rear of the room, making it appear off balance.

It is interesting to note that the main bedding is made up of

The addition of one item of furniture or fabric can have a profound effect on a room. This oriental chest, for example, would certainly set the tone of a bedroom. Imagine how different the bedroom featured opposite would appear if the bedding were replaced with a different style of cover.

Modern anglepoise lamps and metal sculptures team perfectly with traditional patterns and designs of Africa and Australasia. An eclectic mix – the style works well because the lines, images and colours are vivid and bold.

black, cream, brown and mustard. Although this combination adds depth to the room, it does not contribute to the warmth that the scheme obviously has. Instead, the designer has cleverly introduced warm red tones into the room via a cushion in the centre of the bed (it also contains the other, earthy, bed cover colours), and an abstract painting hanging above it. When these combine with the naturally mellow tones of the mahogany furniture scattered around the bedroom, they add the level of warmth the colour scheme needs.

Old meets new to create a classical effect

A first-floor drawing room in a typically tall turn-of-the-last-century town house has been given a simple, streamlined look, without losing its basic architectural character. The tall, elegant casement windows that open onto a balcony are dominant features, an impression that is emphasized by the picture and occasional table placed between them. The windows themselves have been treated very simply, with sheer drapes thrown over a pole to create swags and floor-length tails. A basic roller blind underneath can be pulled down for night time privacy, or on summer days to reduce the sun's glare.

The colour scheme of this living room is a cool, neutral cream. With such large windows, the end result is a spacious airiness. To prevent the room from appearing too cool, the original pine floorboards have been retained. They were stripped and re-sealed and the warm, honey-coloured end result is a perfect foil for the walls and soft furnishings. If your floorboards are not in especially good condition, consider liming or painting them. Either of these finishes makes a virtue of weatherboards. For a limed effect, brush over a wash of diluted white matt emulsion paint. For an aged effect, sand back the surface.

To add yet more warmth to this room, accent colours have been incorporated. The geometric wall hanging, cushions ranged along the sofa, and the charming floral painting are predominantly red with additional touches of yellow. Both of these colours come from the warm side of the

Cool crisp cotton ticking and soft flowing muslin provide contrasting textures to the hard slate effects and highly polished wood in this contemporary room.

colour wheel and so counterbalance the coolness of the rest of the decor.

A spacious room such as this with a few, well-chosen pieces of furniture benefits from some other accessories. These need not be small. To retain the minimalist, contemporary style, the owners of this particular room have chosen a simple potted tree to help bring the outdoors in and to create an additional spot of colour. In the opposite corner of the room, there is also a rather splendid statue whose peaceful countenance can only bring calm and serenity to all who look at her.

The windows are dressed with the bare minimum of draped muslin, allowing enough natural light to emphasize the contrasting hard, soft and shiny surfaces within the room.

Upbeat style with bold colours

In a bold scheme such as tangerine and turquoise, use fabrics in sympathetic colours but more muted shades, if possible.

Many contemporary schemes rely on the clever use of colour for maximum impact, especially when the budget is tight. This often means choosing complementary colours to create a visually stimulating look. Here turquoise and burnt orange – true complements of each other – have been used to stunning effect. The occasional table is painted pale turquoise to echo the colour of the chair, making it an integral part of the scheme.

The setting is the top floor of a converted house, where an attractive arched window is the focal point. The seating is arranged to capitalize on this, and on the view over the rooftops. The window has been left uncovered as the room is not over-looked, while plants provide a subtle screen – they will thrive in such light conditions. The room divider that separates the dining and sitting area is curved to echo the window shape, and helps to zone the two spaces.

The disparate pieces of furniture have tailored covers in a mix-ture of patterned and plain fabrics, all from the same colour palette, that echo the turquoise, apricot and burnt orange theme. The patterns on the sofa and stool are restrained, which helps to define their individual shapes.

Strong, bold colours work well in a contemporary setting where shapes are uncomplicated and lines are clean.

Being at the top of the building, the ceil-ing of the room is not very high. To make it seem higher, the walls are painted in a soft

golden yellow, a few tones paler than the floor, and the ceiling is
an even lighter tone. This treatment of the main surfaces helps to
create an impression of greater space and height, and unifies the
strongly contrasting turquoise and orange.

Lighting is provided by standard and table lamps, which create
low pools of light, while floor-mounted uplighters are used to cast
light onto the ceiling at night, to help increase its apparent height.
This treatment needs a well-plastered ceiling, otherwise any faults
will be emphasized.

Accessories have been kept to a minimum and relate to the
principal colours in the rest of the scheme.

Such a fresh and zingy colour scheme works especially well when there is plenty of natural daylight flooding into the living room.

Country and cottage style

Interior design is no longer as formal as it once was. Purists would still say, however, that you should only decorate your home in a style in keeping with the age and genre of the property. But when you consider the number of new homes to install Adam-style fireplaces, coving and picture rails over the last few years, you can see that this is a view now only shared by a few designer/decorators. This bedroom, for example, has the proportions and architectural detailing of a typical small family town house, yet the owner has chosen to give it a distinctive country feel. The interesting thing is the way she or he has relied almost totally on paint to create this effect.

If you are decorating on a budget and want to disguise a feature that is not in keeping, such as the fitted wardrobe seen here, consider painting it a colour that will blend into the walls. Avoid adding too much unnecessary detailing.

The floorboards have been stripped and gently limed. This is achieved with a proprietary liming wax, which is applied to the floor using a dry cloth and then any excess is removed with a second, clean, cloth. Alternatively, apply a coat of white emulsion paint diluted three parts water to one part paint to the floor with a paintbrush. Then leave the floor to dry and finish with a clear matt floor wax. Both methods are very effective, but if you are looking for a heavily limed effect, it is better to use the liming wax and first work against the timber grain with a wire brush.

There are now a great many rustic accessories available to buy "new", all of which add nostalgic character to any cottage-style room.

The walls have been painted in stripes of grey and yellow, yet another simple but very effective paint finish. Before starting to paint, measure and mark out the stripes using low-tack masking tape. To achieve the washed-out look that is on these walls, either use a ready-mixed paint effect glaze in your chosen colours or blend emulsion paint with a clear emulsion glaze following the manufacturer's instructions. Apply the paints to the masked areas of wall using an uneven brush stroke and leaving obvious unpainted areas. Once dry, apply a second coat to build up the soft, cloudy effect.

A collection of antique and reproduction white linen adds grace to any country house bedroom.

Finally, the bed has been given a distressed finish on which areas have then been stencilled and decorated using gilding wax. The cost of decoration here is minimal, but with a few country pieces of furniture, the room is very effective.

Welcoming warmth with muted colours and soft lighting

If you are without a mantelpiece and want to create something similar, search out a simple shelving unit and display ceramics, glass, or any other objects that you cherish.

The rustic look perfectly complements this country cottage interior, being typical of the timber-framed buildings of hundreds of years ago. This method of building construction is becoming popular again and is well worth considering if you want to create a rustic-style living space.

The ceiling beams are exposed and matt sealed. (Never paint, stain or creosote old beams as this spoils their natural texture and colour.) A mantelshelf is added above the fireplace to tone. The chimney breast and walls are simply plastered and painted off-white — as is the plaster between the ceiling beams — with the brick interior of the fireplace left exposed.

Individual pieces of comfortable upholstered furniture are gathered around this inviting focal point, and are covered in different fabrics. The simple striped woven stool cover, the striped and coordinating floral chintzes on the small armchair and ample, buttoned sofa work well together. Conventional three-piece suites and a collection of all-matching items do not work if you want to create a rustic look.

The original tiled floor is covered in oriental rugs — dyed in warm, earthy colours — to provide comfort underfoot. When used on hard floors, such rugs should always have a non-slip backing to prevent "creeping and curl" and to avoid accidents. If the rugs are coloured using natural dyes, a backing will prevent staining of the floor beneath.

A very inviting living room has been created through soft and comfortable furnishings, a plethora of well-positioned pictures and other accessories, and subtle lighting.

The accessories are chosen to further enhance the rustic theme. The pictures on coloured mounts, all similarly framed, draw attention to the fireplace. The circular occasional tables are covered with textured woven throws, in similar colours to the upholstered stool, and are used to display a cherished collection.

When the lamps are lit, they cast pools of light onto these objects, highlighting the pictures mounted on the chimney breast, and bathing the entire seating area in a warm and very welcoming glow.

Soft velvets, brocades and fringed braids in muted colours are hallmarks of the country look.

Homely look in an old-fashioned kitchen

Pine is one of the timbers most often associated with the cottage interior, and there is still a large choice of pine furniture available, the majority of which is reproduction. With the revival of interest in pine furniture over the past decade or so, most of the original pieces were quickly snapped up. Fortunately, there are now a number of manufacturers using traditional methods to produce excellent pieces of furniture from reclaimed timber. These make a perfectly acceptable substitute, while having the benefit of being available to order in any shape and size imaginable. This makes the job of creating a practical and authentic-looking cottage kitchen ever simpler.

Originally, only free-standing pieces of furniture would have been found in the cottage kitchen, but nowadays a careful blend of both fitted and unfitted pieces can fulfil the needs of the modern family without straying too far from a traditional style of decor. The back-to-basics feel of a traditional cottage can also be retained by concealing all the modern appliances behind the unit fronts.

The cooking range is a dominant feature in the traditional cottage kitchen. There are now a number of 'traditional'-style cookers available, inspired by the popularity of solid fuel and gas-powered enamelled ranges. Originally, the range was both a reliable cooking appliance and a source of heat for the home. The new wave of gas and electric cookers, however, are purely a cooking facility. The positioning of the traditional enamelled range was restricted because it needed to be vented — it would have been placed close to an outside wall. Today, power flues can be used to

Old-fashioned enamelled tinware and china can be bought quite inexpensively to complete the country look.

Traditional accessories and clutter are all part of the character associated with a cottage-style kitchen. No matter how confined the space – and country kitchens by their very nature are small – be sure to have a goodly mix of china, enamelled tinware and nostalgic paraphernalia.

Check fabrics have long been associated with country-style decor. Use them to make simple curtains and pelmets for the window, or to cover unsightly areas that lurk below the sink.

draw the fumes a greater distance, giving modern kitchen designers more flexibility when planning.

The kitchen featured here not only uses traditional materials, like pine, and products such as the cooking range and the Belfast sink, but it also uses traditional colours to evoke the nostalgia of an old-fashioned cottage kitchen. Buttermilk walls give the room a warmth reminiscent of age-stained paintwork, while deep bottle green adds an impression of depth and definition to the colour scheme.

Recreating the rustic charm of the cottage kitchen

Antique pine and moss green woodwork are hallmarks of the country kitchen. The old-fashioned stoneware, the range and marble-topped butcher's block contribute to the look.

To the traditionalists among us, the word "cottage" conjures up images of rustic timber, time-worn stone, quarry floors, and back-to-basics furnishings and fittings. To the more adventurous, however, the idea of the cottage interior offers the opportunity of creating a room with traditional cottage features mixed with more contemporary elements, complementary to a rural setting.

Regardless of their individual elements, cottage kitchens have a welcoming, unpretentious air. This is perpetuated by natural products and home-spun fabrics. The last few years have seen a surge in the popularity of distressed painted furniture, and rustic flooring; even modern paint finishes now emulate aged plaster walls. These contemporary elements are successfully used in the most modern of rooms. But because of their origins, they also work very well in a cottage environment. Therefore, it comes as no surprise to find a new wave of interiors incorporating these interpretations of traditional items.

The one thing they all have in common is their natural properties. Wrought iron is the perfect example: this is a traditional product and would have featured in the cottage kitchen in forged door furniture and the cooking range. Nowadays it can be seen as contemporary dining furniture and accessories. Likewise, there has been a resurgence in natural paints such as distemper and limewash, which bring an atmosphere of greater authenticity to the cottage kitchen of today.

BELOW: Contemporary
elements like modern paint
colours and paint techniques
sit perfectly in this traditional
cottage kitchen. The overwhelming feeling is one of
cosy comfort and natural,
rustic charm.

LEFT: Exposed beams make
an architectural statement in
a cottage kitchen. New 'fake'
beams can give the illusion
of a traditional form of
construction inside the most
modern properties.

Vibrant colours for a fresh look

A country styled room need not appear dusty and drab or frilly and twee, modern colours and techniques can be employed to provide a successful rustic setting. The secret is to use items that would originally have been found in the pure form of that style of room, but use them in new, vibrant colours or designs, adding a twist to a traditional decorative style.

Here, whitewashed walls and wooden floorboards are the basic backdrop for the soft furnishings and furniture. As you would expect, the bed is traditional wrought iron but in a modern scroll design. In place of lace and patchwork, a contemporary quilt and cover dresses the bed in a crisp, traditional yellow and blue deckchair stripe, and as an effective replacement to fussy bed drapes, a simple length of blue sheer fabric is hung over the back of the bed. There is a coolness that accompanies a blue fabric, giving any room a calm atmosphere. But the yellow contrast adds a little welcome warmth to this particular room. Yellow is also evident in the attractive floral fabric used to dress the simple window.

As with any room using almost equal amounts of two colours, plus a non-colour such as white, there is the need for a little something extra to act as an accent to give the colour scheme more of a lift. Here, the accent is supplied by the curtain fabric which contains greens and reds in addition to the shades of blue and yellow.

A modern piece of furniture can work well in a country setting if it is softened with a matt paint or a distressed paint effect.

A simple tabbed heading has also been chosen for the curtains, which slightly brush the floor, softening the hard lines where the wall meets the floor. These have been hung from a wrought iron curtain pole, once again a modern trend but nevertheless with its origins in the past.

As with all well-decorated rooms, the accessories here are chosen to enhance the style of decoration. Fresh flowers grace the window-ledge and side table, and a simply painted chair offers a seat for looking onto the garden.

Many styles of wrought iron curtain pole are available, varying from the simple shepherd's crook to the more ornate split and twisted finial.

Floral fabrics work particularly well when teamed with checks or stripes.

A symphony of florals brings a breath of the country

All carefully designed rooms have a starting point from which the other decorative features are inspired, creating a pleasing harmony without looking over co-ordinated. In this comfortable, country-style en-suite bathroom, a fresh floral curtain fabric, borrowed from the adjoining bedroom, is the inspiration for soft, relaxing creams, ochres, jade and moss pink.

Selecting suitable shades and transferring them to other furnishings introduces interesting textural contrasts too. Thanks to their complementary colour palette, this duet of wallpapers happily combines country small-print floral with an elegantly striped panelling effect below the dado rail. Old-fashioned framed prints and fresh flowers continue the flowery theme. A luxuriant moss pink and cream rug has been laid on rough and ready, jade-stained stripped boards, a practical as well as a visually exciting choice, while cushions on the window-seat pick up the pink and green colouring.

The use of papers, fabrics, rugs and cushions have successfully softened the effect of what can sometimes be a rather cold and impersonal room. But the finishing touches are the dark gleam of mahogany and the shine of brass taps, cleverly matched to the picture frames,

These lime-washed shelves provide easily accessible storage for small items and add decorative detail to a country-style bathroom.

Bring the country garden inside with these pretty wirework plant holders.

which add life and light to the whole room.

The rest of the furniture is dark, polished wickerwork, the perfect foil for the softer upholstered elements, yet a good companion for the mahogany. In order to maintain a sense of relaxation and cottage-style informality, the bath area has been partially screened by a partition wall and elegant archway. This avoids that vast expanse of empty space that leaves so many bathrooms desolate, and provides an extra vertical surface for a pretty washbasin and mirror.

Clever colour scheming and pleasantly contrasting textures have given this cosy bathroom a rustic air.

Country and town house kitchen

Reproduction antique French-style dining chairs grace the dining table in this kitchen. Note how well they blend with traditional practical elements like the plate rack and simple wall-mounted shelves.

Unlike the true cottage interior, based on the home of the farmworker or smallholder, country and town house styles fall somewhere between grand and rustic. Traditionally, many country house owners also had a house in the town, which is where the crossover of style originates. The owners were richer than their country cottage neighbours, so the furniture purchased for such houses was grander – yet subject to the decorative trends of the day – while still blending in perfectly with a country style of furnishing, such as a full-blown rose chintz fabric.

The country house kitchen originally offered the occupant the best design that money could buy, but in a distinctly more casual style than in the town house. Many of the larger country houses had lavishly equipped kitchens with walls of built-in storage and generous range cookers. This is where the traditional fitted kitchen originated, finished in either natural timber or painted in simple colours, as it still is in many turn-of-the-century houses.

These kitchens were designed to be practical, with hard-wearing stone or quarry tiled floors, and large pine or scrubbed oak tables. Elements such as these can still be seen in the country house styled kitchen, but as these rooms are not purely for the use of food preparation, they may be blended with the somewhat grander kinds of furniture found in other rooms around the home.

BELOW: Painted traditional kitchen units have a more formal appearance than their pine or oak alternatives, ideal for reproducing this particular style of kitchen.

LEFT: Traditional rural features like rustic flooring, pressed tiles and basket-ware are teamed with a smart painted kitchen to produce a more formal country house style.

Traditional wood takes centre stage for country elegance

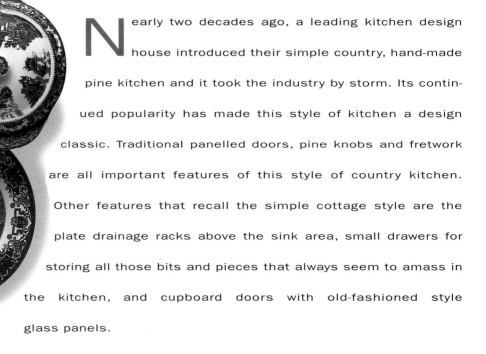

Rustic brick and traditional blue and white china are key elements in the country-style kitchen. If you are unable to expose natural brickwork, modern brick cladding is actually a very realistic alternative.

Nearly two decades ago, a leading kitchen design house introduced their simple country, hand-made pine kitchen and it took the industry by storm. Its continued popularity has made this style of kitchen a design classic. Traditional panelled doors, pine knobs and fretwork are all important features of this style of country kitchen. Other features that recall the simple cottage style are the plate drainage racks above the sink area, small drawers for storing all those bits and pieces that always seem to amass in the kitchen, and cupboard doors with old-fashioned style glass panels.

Rustic timbers feature heavily in the design of this kitchen, both as beams on the ceiling and as supporting upright posts, giving the kitchen an authentic appearance. If your kitchen is not of this period, introducing fake timbers can set the scene.

A flagstone floor is both practical and beautiful, and in this case it blends with the exposed rustic brickwork. There is a wide range of flooring tiles available and if you can't run to the expense of original stone tiles, cushioned flooring is a good imitation — and it is warmer underfoot, too. If you want to use brick in your kitchen, as here, a secondhand brick is the best for this setting as its mellow tones complement the woodwork and the slightly crumbled edges have a worn softness not found in modern bricks.

Above the preparation area an old-fashioned rack — often used for airing clothes — holds saucepans and cookware. It is both practical and a charming decorative feature.

Finally, there is the traditional cooking range, housed in a brick arched recess, reminiscent of the inglenook fireplaces of years gone by. This traditional cooking appliance is the main feature of the kitchen, emphasizing the fact that the cottage kitchen represents the heart of the home, where the family gathers by the warmth of the range to be fed good, hearty, home-produced meals. Today's ranges are available in a far greater number of colours than in years gone by, making them traditional and yet also contemporary in their feel.

An authentic touch: antique copper saucepans hanging from the wall or an overhead rack. Buy reproduction pans if you can't get original ones.

The attractive scrolls running up each of the units draw together the disparate elements in this kitchen.

Old and new features team up for practicality and style

This beautiful painted kitchen looks as though it has evolved lovingly over a period of years. Instead, it is an excellent example of a contemporary painted kitchen which incorporates both traditional and modern features. For example, the square panelling and inset drawer fronts — teamed with details such as the plate rack and free-standing dresser — are in the traditional mode. However, there are also elements of the built-in kitchen (the run of worktops, the cooker hood) that, together with contemporary paint techniques and colours, create an overall effect that is far from rustic.

Generally, the room has the feel of a totally free-standing kitchen, even though the majority of the units are fitted. This is achieved by keeping the run of worktops and base units to a minimum. Breaks in continuity, however small, create groups of units that act like selected individual pieces. For example, the housing for the extractor fan is attached to two small side units, whereas the plate rack is separated from its adjacent unit. Varying surface levels has the same effect, and adds extra interest to the layout. The ceramic tiles, too, are kept to a block confined to the area around the cooking zone, as opposed to running along the length of the worktops, as is more usual.

When you look at the pieces in detail, both the dresser and the main working area include identical design details — even the same handles. But by changing the colour of the units, the effect is that of

Yellow and blue complement each other so beautifully that in a kitchen that features mellow timber and wicker baskets, blue paintwork and furnishings provide the perfect backdrop.

individual pieces of furniture, with different characters. This helps the kitchen to appear as if it has developed gradually rather than having been clinically manufactured. The dresser does not look isolated, however, as the strong blue colour is cleverly echoed in the cupboard linings on the open units and also features in the ceramic tiles.

A quick and simple way to alter the feel of a kitchen is by changing the drawer and door knobs. These usually screw in and out very easily. Imagine how this kitchen would look if the knobs were much larger, or were made of brass or ceramic.

The room has a calm, slightly mellow feel due to the chosen flooring: stone, featuring flashes of warm peach and charcoal colours.

Tranquil style

It's a technique used to great effect in gardens: here a strictly limited colour scheme generates a sense of well-being and tranquility in an attic bathroom. A simple modern white suite and plain painted walls have kept the cost down and emphasized a lofty ceiling to encourage a feeling of peacefulness.

Yet, for all its soaring spaciousness, the room has a cosy, even luxurious atmosphere as a result of the inspired choice of caramel for that large expanse of wall. It is warm and strong without being demanding, as is the bathroom's biggest extravagance: a specially commissioned deep-pile white carpet with co-ordinated caramel fish border. Selective spending is an excellent way to balance the budget when you are seeking the luxury look.

Soap, towels, the simplest mirror and picture frames, even the starfish used as a decorative accessory, have all adhered to this strict two-tone scheme and helped to make this a room to relax in.

Tucked into an alcove and lit by an overhead skylight, even the position of the bath makes the user feel pampered and private. You could recreate this effect whatever shape room you have by boxing in the bath with floor-to-ceiling panels, or shelves and cupboards, and using recessed downlighters in the ceiling above. This might be a useful way to conceal all your plumbing, too.

If the extra space for a bigger, better bathroom isn't available,

A wall-hung basin provides excellent storage space beneath to reduce surface clutter and conceal the pipework.

Keep all the fittings and furnishings to a soft, two-tone colour scheme to maintain an atmosphere of calm.

consider repositioning the existing suite within the room, or replacing some of the items as and when you have the funds. A smaller or corner-fitting bath, or a wall-hung basin, may create a little extra space and a lot more style.

Honeyed tones teamed with simple shapes and a plain white suite and accessories, have brought peace and order to this relaxing bathroom.

Choose blue to be cool, calm and collected

Despite its reputation for being cold and unwelcoming, blue can work brilliantly in the bathroom provided you choose your shades carefully. Here soft petrol blue is teamed with a strong eggshell blue, to create a cool, sophisticated look that both soothes and stimulates.

This bold scheme has taken its lead from the colours on a dramatic, geometrically patterned, cotton rug, seemingly flung casually across the neutral background of wall-to-wall sisal matting. In fact, the rug is an important element in the overall design from other perspectives, too. It links the different items of bathroom furniture across what would otherwise be a rather blank expanse of floor; it has inspired not just the colour scheme for the room, but also its modernist style.

It takes a cool head to keep things simple and add colour in just the right places. If you lack the necessary confidence, try

starting with a "blank canvas". Pare the room down to its basic neutrals: the whites, the woods, the chrome or brass, then gradually add your chosen colour in small doses until you reach the saturation you are happy with. That way you can stop in time if you feel it might spoil the effect.

Don't expect always to get it

Blue inset tiles and a blue painted bath combine to produce a cool, clean feel.

right first time. It sometimes takes a lot of trial and error to find the right colour that performs the way you want it under all conditions. Some shades change dramatically in real or artificial lighting conditions; others can look very different on a vertical or horizontal surface. A matt or shiny finish can also make a tremendous amount of difference. Many of the paint ranges nowadays offer sample pots of different colours and these can be a useful way to avoid expensive mistakes.

Taking the trouble to get a colour just right is well worth the effort when you see the end result. Use a self-mix paint selection if you can't find exactly the shade you want from standard ranges.

Shades of cool green create a restful retreat

Stylish and practical is the way this room is best described. Almost every element has been chosen for its form and function, and all you could possibly need in the bedroom is catered for here.

First and foremost, there is the simple bed that lacks the fussiness of a headboard or bed drapes. Then there is the storage – a wardrobe with its green stained wooden doors – and, finally, a blanket chest positioned beneath a single shelf, which in itself offers an additional storage and display area. This restful,

The European atmosphere in this bedroom has been evoked by the shutters at the windows and the refreshingly pale walls and the soft furnishings. The finished setting is both delightfully fresh and serene.

uncluttered room must surely make for peaceful living.

The floor covering is equally practical. The hard wooden floor has been successfully softened with a large rug to add some warmth underfoot. The natural materials bring life to the room and the neutral tones blend most harmoniously with the *eau-de-Nil* walls.

The wooden shutters create a wonderful filtered light and offer privacy without the addition of colour or pattern that curtains would provide. However, notice how a hint of softness, in the form of softly draped muslin, has been added above the shutters. This touch of romance just breaks up the hard lines that might otherwise detract from the overall atmosphere of this room.

Finishing touches like a large mirror, a comfortable chair, and a small display table, complete the list of practical 'must haves' for a plain bedroom. However, uncluttered living need not necessarily mean bare living, and the soft furnishings comfortably redress the balance. The piped cushions on the chair make it most welcoming and the ties at the top of the back cushion are attractive – and, of course, practical – decorative details. Without them, the cushions would be far too liable to slip around. Likewise, the lace-trimmed pillows add a little luxury to the bedding. The lightweight cotton throw and zigzag, lacy edging on the bed valance tone in beautifully with the walls and this pale, pale shade of green maintains the bedroom's light and airy, and above all, calm ambience.

Simple pale green and off-white paints can add serenity to a room in a way that few other colours can hope to achieve.

Calm and comfort created by neutral colours

Throughout this book you will see some wonderful examples of neutral colour schemes. Part of the joy of using these colours is that because they are so versatile, they look equally at home in a traditional or a contemporary setting. So, to set the theme, make use of the furniture and accessories.

The beautiful room featured opposite has both traditional and contemporary elements that combine to create a very individual and restful environment. The stylish wrought iron bed and occasional pieces of furniture are suitably traditional and they contrast nicely with the refreshing approach to soft furnishings that has been adopted. While bed canopies and curtain pelmets are all a part of the traditional school of decorating, not a frill or a swag is on display here. Instead, a mixture of patterned and plain fabrics add detail.

A practical quilt cover and valance (which is easy to remove, and easy to wash) have been chosen to dress the bed, and with the addition of throws in various tones and designs, and crisp simple cushions, the effect is restful yet decidedly sumptuous.

The room is not particularly large, yet it has a very high and shapely ceiling. Note the tricks the designer has used to reduce the appearance of its height. The window, for example, is tall and narrow but because the curtains are the same colour and tone as the walls this is not exaggerated as it would

Mixing natural coloured fabrics gives you the opportunity to make the most of design details. The satin edging and pompoms used on these wonderful cushions add interest but take nothing away from the overall harmonious look.

Aged or distressed pieces of wooden furniture have a softness to them that works particularly well in a tranquil interior.

be with curtains of a deeper colour or tone. Furthermore, with the addition of a Roman blind, the window height is subtly reduced, giving the whole wall a better proportion. The carefully positioned pictures also help to draw the eye line downwards, as does the bed drape: its generous band of fabric hangs down towards the front of the bed.

In a small bedroom, choose your occasional furniture carefully. It should be practical and offer additional storage, but without overpowering the look of the room.

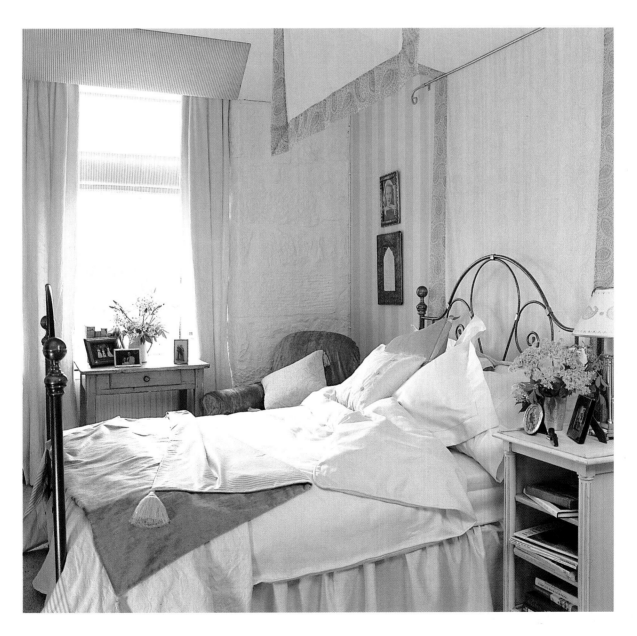

Shaker simplicity
equals tranquility

The name Shaker derives from an American sect founded in 1747. Their individual approach to design produced a truly functional range of furniture and furnishings which lacked ornamentation and decoration. This style has once again become popular, and simple, well-designed and practical rooms can be created in this truly contemporary style.

All the elements in a Shaker bedroom are functional, so your eye is drawn to shape and proportion rather than colour or decorative detail. Despite this emphasis on function and simplicity, a Shaker room lacks nothing in a design sense.

Shaker interiors can be nothing but simple. The belief in purity and simplicity extended from the Shakers' form of worship into the styling of their homes and furnishings.

Plain walls are an integral part of this style of decor, with natural fabrics and both painted and natural wood playing a very important part. Any well-made piece of furniture with graceful lines works well in this setting, as do fabrics such as muslin, gingham, linen and cotton. If you feel the need for pattern, use simple checks and stripes and keep floral prints to a minimum. Opt, too, for muted shades.

The colours used here are soft and there is nothing jarring in the scheme, so the room has a tranquil atmosphere. The colours of both walls and floor appear in the soft furnishings, giving a harmony to the space. The shutters give the room privacy, but simple off-white blinds or curtains would have been a successful alternative if you were looking for something a little softer. Note the detailing on the curtain at the head of the bed. The tabbed heading creates soft folds in the fabric without a fussy gathered effect, and although it is quite plain, it is an extremely effective piece of detailing in the room.

Fresh flowers in an earthenware jug add just a splash of colour, together with the other simple accessories on either side of the bed: the vine and lavender wreath bound with a short length of gingham ribbon and the terracotta jug standing on the chest of drawers. Finally, no Shaker look would be complete without the most well-known of Shaker items — the oval timber boxes. Here they are stacked neatly on the table by the window.

This traditional Shaker box is larger than the standard storage boxes and is designed specifically for containing laundry.

When choosing fabrics, look for designs that feature the same colours used in different ways. This can add variety within unity.

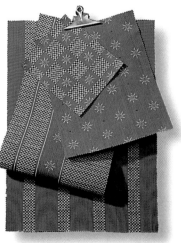

Cool, calming white in a country interior

In this all-neutral rustic setting, the look is one of a Tuscan farmhouse – a cool retreat from the hot summer sun. The wood of the ceiling beams and recess shelves has been bleached to creamy whiteness; the walls are painted plaster and the floors, doors and window frames have been left natural.

This monochromatic scheme helps to create an impression of space and elegance in a fairly confined area, and can be warmed up, or cooled down further, by the addition of specific colour accents and accessories. Depending on your preferences, consider draping a brightly coloured throw casually over one of the

White on cream is not a colour combination that immediately springs to mind, but actually white looks crisper when set against cream.

chairs; add piles of cushions — or perhaps just one, jewel-bright bolster — to the sofa; introduce a wall hanging, or display a collection of objects gleaned from your travels.

The upholstered furniture in this living room relies on an unusual shape — clearly defined by plain covers — to add visual impact, which is echoed in the large stoneware pots filled with rustic twigs. The covers for the furniture are loose fitting for ease of care and yet also tailored to give the neat finish that is the essence of this room.

The subtlest of pattern interest is added in the checked and striped throws, and some muted colour in the terracotta planters. Apart from that, the living room is created around the interplay of different textures: worn wood abounds, the fabric is all self-patterned and the terracotta pots have the wonderful patina of age. Even the walls have retained their pitty, lumpy surfaces. Distemper paint, which is becoming increasingly easy to buy, is the perfect foil for walls such as these. Distemper creates a permeable surface and so does not trap damp in aging walls.

This more sophisticated version of the rustic look could be recreated almost anywhere, in town or country, and would be particularly effective in a seaside or ocean setting. On a practical note, very pale schemes and upholstery are not especially suitable for family living. Good interior design must allow for a combination of the practical and the aesthetic.

Branches collected in mid-winter and displayed in a simple white container with florist's foam are a striking addition to an interior such as this. The foam is concealed with scrunched-up tissue paper.

Relaxing setting adds spice with animal print accents

Black and white patterns are supremely striking when set in a simple, monochromatic colour scheme.

Subtle patterns are introduced through the patina of natural timber, textiles and fruits.

This style can be used to create a room in which it is easy to relax after a hard day's work. The seating is arranged in a comfortable U-shape, to ease conversation, and grouped around a low level coffee table, which is also used for storage. The coffee table, positioned in front of the seating, is an essential part of the style, and was adapted in the 1950s from a sofa table (which used to be positioned at the back, or drawn up to the side of the sofa for games, say, or to support lamps).

The soft, neutral colours give an impression of space and cool calm. The beiges, creams and off-whites with bleached woods rely on interesting textures and sharply defined contrast of form, to create a stylish sitting room. Even the radiator is coloured to blend unobtrusively into the background. If you choose to paint your radiator to match the background wall, avoid oil-based paints as the colours will discolour and stain in the course of time.

Pattern in this contemporary setting is restrained, being confined to an upholstered chair and two geometric abstract pictures, which are not particularly dominant as they are all part of the monochromatic scheme, and thus blend into the background. Instead, tonal contrast is achieved by the darker floor colour, strikingly contrasting patterned cushions and stripped natural wood window frames – a model of understatement.

The window treatment, too, is simple, with neat, narrow-slatted 'micro' blinds that can be angled to diffuse the daylight. Night lighting is provided by pools of light cast from the lamps on the glass storage chests to each side of the sofa, and by wall-washers, which bathe the paintings in a warm glow. Houseplants are used to provide a crisp green accent — very much an integral part of the Scandinavian look.

Soft, neutral colours create a sense of calm and peace. Mix beige, buttermilk and oyster colours with bleached woods, using accessories such as plants to provide contrasts.

Cool blue creates a contemporary feel

Checks and plaids will always add character to a room and are the perfect way to introduce tonal variation or an accent or two.

A kitchen like this one is very versatile. Depending on the colour in which it is painted and the surrounding decor, it can take on a variety of different looks. Here, shades of soft blue and terracotta have been carefully combined to create a simple and contemporary atmosphere.

The pale blue gives the room a calm, uncluttered air, and as it is teamed with an off-white, it is also deliciously soft. The floor is covered with linoleum in a practical, pale terracotta shade that is linked to the rest of the kitchen with its blue inserts. The colour of these is deeper than the units, supplying a variation of tone, and therefore a dimension to the decor. The colour of the floor is then lifted into the main scheme via the introduction of a terracotta bowl and a picture framed in natural wood. Earth colours like these blend especially well with Mediterranean shades of blue, pink and white.

Specially purchased kitchenware should be seen, and not hidden away. With so many well-designed pieces now available at affordable prices, why not display them for all to see?

The gingham Roman blind over the French windows adds a splash of colour to the kitchen, too: checks and plaids have a wonderful traditional quality. The simplicity of the blind combined with the freshness of the gingham means that colour is injected but without detracting from the airy quality of this kitchen. By using the gingham elsewhere, such as in napkins or chair seats, for example, the fabric could also be used to add further tonal variation in the room.

While the walls and the kitchen units are painted the same

colour, important tonal variations are supplied by the blue glass-ware. The incidental basket of lemons near the French windows adds an accent to the room, as the vibrant yellow contrasts so strongly with the essentially blue colour scheme. The room design also benefits greatly from the kitchenware. It is such a shame to hide away well designed pieces: if they have been chosen to enhance your kitchen, display them for all to see.

The calm serenity of this kitchen is achieved by the blending of soft blue with simple off-white. The basket of lemons and bowl of plums are a charmingly natural way of using colour accents.

Children's rooms

Achild's bedroom tends to be the area where the designer feels most confident in using decorative elements such as murals and decoupage. Of course, many people will avoid trying this themselves unless they have experience in decorative painting but, as this room shows, some of the simplest painted motifs can have a wonderful effect and need only limited ability and just a little confidence. Here, a sailing motif has been chosen to decorate this fully-fitted bedroom furniture and, to add drama to the scheme, a freehand wave has been painted around the bed and continued into the room at dado height.

Blue will always make a room's floor area appear much larger, and when used with yellow produces a bright and sunny room.

The bedroom is completely furnished in simple two-tone grey fitted furniture incorporating a captain's bed. This offers extensive storage, and is made from a hard-wearing and easy-to-clean material, a must in a room like this. There is a desk for homework and a pull-out unit at the bedside offering a versatile area at which the occupant can play or put night-time drinks or books. Fitted furniture gives the opportunity of producing a very well-organized bedroom but can look a little hard and clinical at times. Here, though, the furniture design incorporates many different levels. This helps to break up the hard lines, making the layout more relaxed and casual.

It is hard to tell if this decorative scheme was chosen with the furniture in mind or if the furniture was chosen first and then the captain's bed was the inspiration for the nautical scheme. The room could look quite different if the grey surrounds on the furniture were replaced with white or blue on a soft grey base. This would then provide a more integrated colour scheme rather than the contrasting one shown here. Check with furniture manufacturers who can usually offer a choice of "trims".

There are some other, very attractive, decorative details. For example, the border running along the top of the walls has also been used to create a pelmet at the top of the window, and the boat motifs embellish the furniture. These all add interest and, coupled with the red accessories, give life to the scheme.

Children's bedrooms will always benefit from movable storage such as these plastic containers on castors. Not only are they useful but the bright colours will also add extra detail to a room.

Warm colours create an attic haven

An child's attic bedroom is often full of character and interesting shapes and detailing, but, of course, these details can bring with them their own unique design problems. One of the most common is where, design-wise, in a room with sloping ceilings, should the walls end and the ceiling begin? Should you risk taking one finish over the whole room, or is there a possibility that this will appear to reduce the ceiling height? To prevent that from happening in this room, the timber cladding across the ceiling has been painted in a gloss white, as its reflective quality adds both light and height. Furthermore, the width of the room has been maximized by running the timber cladding right across the ceiling and down the wall to the left. The horizontal lines add visual width to the room.

The basic colour scheme has been designed to be simple and to offer a welcoming warm glow. This is achieved with the use of quite a powerful apricot paint on the walls and with the addition of the mellow timber flooring and furniture. While it is tempting to use light colours in dark, small rooms, if the room lacks natural light, delicate colours and patterns will take on a faded and insipid appearance having very little, if any, impact. This leaves the room fundamentally dull and uninteresting. Instead, such spaces need depth of colour to offer character and brightness, and colours from the warm side of the colour

By changing the style of a window dressing, the whole atmosphere of a room is changed. Imagine what the bedroom opposite would look like if the window featured this softly draped blind instead of the more linear blind it is currently sporting.

wheel, such as terracotta, cherry red and primrose yellow, are perfect.

Accessories are kept to a minimum here, ensuring the room looks as uncluttered as possible, but those used have been carefully chosen. For example, the coat peg on the left-hand wall gives storage for bags and coats, and the box beneath the window is in a similar tone to the walls, and does not match the remaining furniture. This ensures the area looks as open as possible, making the window – with its simple blind – the centre of attention in that part of the room.

Your choice of pictures can add to the colour scheme of a room. Notice how the colours of the subject matter and frames on the two pictures above the bed pick up the furniture tone and colours in the rug.

Ice cream pink bedroom for a little girl

This soft strawberry and cream room acts as the perfect backdrop for a colourful bed cover and toys. The walls have been divided with a dado rail which is decorated below with cream and pink stripes of paint. The decor is simple and a balance is achieved when the paint colour used above the dado is introduced below, via the painted cupboard and storage chest. This is further enhanced by the

This simply decorated little girl's bedroom is the perfect setting for a night of sweet dreams. Pink and cream makes for a very peaceful combination.

colours below being taken above the dado in the form of little bows, the bed drape and also on the mounts around each of the pictures.

The pictures were made by painting or stamping simple motifs onto white card using the deepest colour from the decor. They were then framed and grouped on the wall and successfully enhance the simplicity of the colour scheme. The crown motif has also been enlarged, cut from timber and painted the same colour as the dado rail to create a novel corona for the bed. It has been completed by the simple, sheer drapes falling down to floor level on each side of the bed. The bright quilt cover has been made simply using large appliqué shapes and, if you so desired, you could repeat the motifs used in the pictures on the wall and in suitable toning colours.

A low playing or working area has been created by the small folding table and two children's wicker chairs that have been painted to blend into the scheme. Such miniature furniture is widely available, is easy to paint and is the perfect way to bring a child's eye view into a room. In a room like this, the brightly coloured toys provide all the colour accents you could possibly need.

Pretty pinks create a softly-coloured bedroom. The touches of green on these cushions give a lift to what might otherwise be too much pink.

Simple motifs like these teddy bears can be introduced to add interest to a bedroom and they can be painted or stamped in any colour to complement your colour scheme.

White and powder blue create a classic nursery style

Call me old-fashioned, but I think that traditionally styled nurseries are the best. They evoke traditional values and add a delicate quality to a room, something which cannot be achieved with the use of the brightly coloured fabrics that are growing in popularity. The nursery should be a peaceful place but the difficulty in decorating a room like this is that a child will very soon outgrow its decorative style. So unless you can afford to redecorate in a relatively short length of time, consider how you are going to furnish the room very carefully.

Pastels work best in a traditional setting, and you can either plump for the more usual shades of blue for a boy and pink for a girl, or for something a little different, such as aquamarine and yellow. Here, baby blue and pink have been used to create a soft interior, which has a very calm, serene atmosphere because the blue dominates. The principal wallpaper showing a blue goose design has been used up to dado height with a white background paper featuring a small pink motif above. This gives the illusion of height in what is quite a low bedroom.

In a room of this size, too much pattern would be overpowering, so the designer has cleverly employed plain white for curtaining and soft furnishings. The lace-edged curtains and valance that dress the window have been gathered with smocking. This can be achieved either by traditional smocking methods or with the use of a commercially bought tape. This detail has been echoed in the tiebacks, and on the cleverly positioned bed drapes. The angle of the ceiling has been used to great effect here with

the bed drapes hung directly from tracks attached to the ceiling. This technique can also be used to create half-testers (see p.164), and four-posters for full-sized beds in attic or dormer bed-rooms. With nurseries, however, be aware of the style of tieback used to secure the drapes as they should be kept short to avoid the risk of strangulation should they work loose.

The main items needed for a nursery are a safe place in which the baby can sleep, a chest or small cupboard for storage and a comfortable chair for nursing and night-time feeds. Even the smallest of rooms should contain all these.

Fun, flexible style lets the room grow with the child

There is one main difference between a child's bedroom and any other in the house, and that is the child's room should grow with the child. So unless your budget will allow you to redesign the room periodically, keep the decorative scheme flexible, allowing you to change elements to give the room a new design perspective as the child matures.

Most nurseries are decorated to please the parents and not the child. With the exception of supplying a safe, warm environment that offers ample storage for clothing and necessities, the young baby does not necessarily benefit from the decorative borders, pretty papers and frilly curtains that many parents install into their child's first bedroom.

The design challenge begins when you are decorating for the toddler upwards, as their needs change so quickly from being a safe haven in which to play and sleep, to an area in which to study, entertain friends and relax. This, coupled with their liking and disliking of certain types of designs and trends, makes the job of decorating much more complex. To make life as simple as possible, design the room around a limited range of colours and let the accessories change over the years to reflect your child's current likes and dislikes.

For a child's room that grows with them, avoid film or TV character bed linen as these can quickly date. Instead, use fresh checks and bright cottons which are easy to launder. For embellishment, stencil a teddy border on the wall or headboard and add teddy buttons to cushions or pillows.

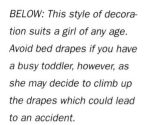

BELOW: This style of decoration suits a girl of any age. Avoid bed drapes if you have a busy toddler, however, as she may decide to climb up the drapes which could lead to an accident.

LEFT: This furniture offers ample storage and an additional play area which can be removed or turned into a work area as the child grows. There are many styles of cabin bed like this from which to choose.

Fun for the family and practical too

When you have a young family, bathtime is fun-time, which can be reflected in your choice of decoration. If you have a separate bathroom or shower room for the children, this is an even better excuse to go wild with strong colours, bold patterns and cheerful motifs.

This small shower room has a deceptively spacious feel to it, achieved by fitting the narrow cubicle into a recessed cupboard

Children love this bright and cheery shower room, but it's also designed to be safe and easy to clean.

and using a bright royal-blue and sunshine-yellow colour scheme. A starfish mirror, and smiling-sun robe hooks painted to match, have long-lasting appeal for all ages, unlike a popular cartoon or storybook figure that will go out of fashion too quickly. Children grow up so fast, it is far better to keep your ideas bright but simple so that they can be updated easily and economically.

Painted furniture, storage and accessories for children's rooms can be expensive, but you can buy unpainted wooden "blanks" by mail order, and finish them in whatever colour and style you fancy. If you are not very good at painting pictures, then try decoupage: cutting out pictures and sticking them on, then protecting with several coats of varnish.

Most importantly, a family bathroom or shower room must be safe and practical, it's going to take a lot of punishment! All surfaces must be waterproof and easy to clean. Here, floor-to-ceiling ceramic tiles and tongue-and-groove panelling, treated to a water-resistant paint, simply need a wipe-down to keep them looking good. On the floor, non-slip tiles are protected by a wooden duckboard, so much more comfortable and hygienic to step out of a wet shower onto than a soggy bathmat.

At the window a wipe-clean slatted blind (reflected in the mirror), is a practical alternative to curtains. Even the safety-glass shower door acts on a pivot: it's easy to use, takes up very little space and cannot be flung back against the wall.

Family bathrooms need plenty of open storage for clothes and toys.

These cheeful ceramic pictures are ideal wall decorations for the humid atmosphere of a bathroom.

Vivid colours add vibrancy to a child-centred kitchen

Most families need to find a great deal of space for the many time-saving devices now available, such as the microwave oven, food processor, the juicer, or even the dough-nut maker. A fitted kitchen is the best solution for people who need gener-ous amounts of storage unless, of course, the house has a traditional pantry space. One of the other benefits of fitted kitchens is that they are available in a wide range of styles and finishes, most of which have been designed and manufactured to offer the best in storage and are easy to clean and maintain. This kitchen offers all these benefits, with the addition of a bright, fun and safe environment for the whole family.

The oven is housed within a wall unit ensuring it is out of the reach of the children and also at a level which is easily accessi-ble. Directly above the cooker there is a small microwave oven fitted in one of the cupboards, again out of the children's reach and hidden from view, keeping the kitchen as streamlined as pos-sible. The hob is surrounded by a removable chrome safety guard – a vital safety device to prevent a curious toddler from pulling down a burning pot on his or her head. The controls to the hob are sited above rather than underneath. This clever positioning keeps the controls away from children's ever-inquisitive fingers but at a perfect height for an adult.

In a well-designed fitted kitchen such as this, all other appli-ances such as the refrigerator, freezer and dishwasher can be

This fitted kitchen in light beech and pale green has been specifically planned for a growing family, offering safety features and a streamlined, ergonomic layout to make it pleasant to work in while providing plenty of floor and tabletop space.

installed behind units, in the same way as the microwave. The kitchen remains neat and the appliances hidden.

Decoratively, the light green and pale beech units are the perfect simple backdrop to the brightly coloured accessories that have been chosen to enhance the room. When decorating any room that will regularly house children, do not forget to allow space for all their colourful toys and other bits and pieces.

Vivid colours in modern, translucent plastic or glass light up a primarily neutral-coloured kitchen.

Conservatory and garden rooms

The garden room or conservatory often bridges the gap between the patio, terrace or verandah, and the main living room. It can be a separate extension to the house, used for summer living and dining, possibly filled with exotic plants and shrubs, or it may be an integral part of an existing room. It can be used to create a sense of space and all-year-round summer in a dark, overshadowed living room or gloomy basement.

The decorations, furniture and furnishings may echo the theme of the main living area, or you can create a specific style more in keeping with the traditional conservatory. You may favour a "return to the Raj" look, for example, or a Shaker style with painted and distressed furniture, simple accessories and patchwork fabrics.

If you plan to extend a room in this way, ensure the glazing is adequate to provide good insulation, both from winter cold and summer heat – no one wants to shiver or fry when temperatures drop or soar. Ventilation will need to be carefully controlled, especially if the room is to contain exotic flora, and heating should be equally efficient.

Some form of sun screening will also be essential – there are many companies that specialize in conservatory blinds and awnings. Canvas screening, which unfurls like a yacht sail, can be both practical and decorative.

In a garden room, lighting will have to be incorporated in the structure as discreet fittings. Pools of light, thrown from table lamps and candles are intimate and effective.

RIGHT: Because of its many French windows and simple styling, this living room has the feel of a conservatory. Any room at the back of the house can be remodelled by adding large picture windows or patio doors to create a garden living room.

BELOW: Don't be limited to traditional conservatory furniture. This room is proof that it can look every bit as formal as a more conventional living room.

Casual dining in the conservatory

Casual dining has now become more popular than ever, with many people substituting the traditional dining room in their house for an eating area within, or adjoining, one of the other rooms. A conservatory or garden room makes the perfect setting for such an area, especially on a warm summer's evening or for a sunny lunchtime meal.

This combined kitchen and dining room is home to a traditional solid fuel cooker, yet it retains a very modern feel. The aquamarine and white are a striking and fresh combination working together harmoniously because they are both cool colours. Accents of bright mauve provide contrast.

Garden rooms and conservatories have traditionally been painted white, however with the trend towards using these rooms as year-round areas, they can easily take a more interesting colour scheme. Because of their association with the outdoors, consider decorating in green or blue pastel shades, colours which echo the sky and greenery beyond. Aquamarine provides a refreshing choice, or try lavender blue.

Lavender blue with a touch of peach helps maintain the airy feel of this room yet at the same time adds warmth to the space.

Light and shade – and how to use it successfully

This conservatory extension to a main living area leads out onto a terrace where pale and sunshine colours ensure maximum light is reflected into the darker, original living space. The unusual fan shape of the extension is echoed in the curved form of the sofa and the cane chair, which also provides textural contrast, and is enhanced by the feathery feel of the plants.

Night lighting is carefully considered with strategically-placed spotlights incorporated into the outside wall of the living room. Uplighters are concealed among the larger plants to give a really effective, shadow-torn light as dusk falls. By day, too much light

With an extension like this, the living room is taken directly out into the garden.

can be dazzling in a conservatory and if you are growing plants in there, the resulting heat will be overwhelming. In this room, sun screening is provided by neatly rolled blinds, which are electronically controlled from inside to unfurl individually to cover the glazed roof. As the ceilings of most conservatories are too high to reach comfortably, it is worth investigating the possibility of electronic blinds. There are, however, many other sorts of blinds – consult an expert to give you the pros and cons.

Imaginative use has been made of the original house wall, which is partially retained and used to support a built-in bookcase. Any such structural building work must be done by a professional builder or conservatory contractor, as load-bearing walls will have to be strengthened to support the floors above. This may well involve the insertion of an RSJ (roof strengthening/rolled steel joist). A structural engineer or surveyor will calculate to ensure the joist is strong enough to bear the load.

The addition of a conservatory or garden room extension may require planning permission – one good reason for employing a specialist contractor, as they are usually well versed in local planning rules, and will undertake to apply for permission on your behalf. A visit to your local authority environmental planning department is worthwhile, to check for yourself.

Tubs of green plants bring the outdoors inside. Select natural stoneware or terracotta pots for a more rustic look, or as a stark contrast in a modern setting.

Cloakrooms and shower rooms

An infolding door is extremely economical on space and is a good choice for this Gothic-style dressing room.

They're the smallest rooms in the house, but they are often the ones with the biggest ideas. An extra toilet squeezed in under the stairs, or added to the plans as part of a new utility/kitchen extension; a walk-in shower room little larger than a

cubicle in the corner of the bedroom, at the end of the hall, or even in a redundant airing cupboard — they both provide valuable extra facilities in the minimum of space.

Yet despite their limited size and functional purpose, a lot of thought and creative effort seems to go into their design and decoration. Perhaps we find their modest dimensions less daunting; or their secondary role as an additional facility means we can take greater risks and be more imaginative in our choice of decoration. Such rooms are often treated to dramatic colour schemes such as all-over plum or maroon to make 'them cosier; or a joke theme to make the user smile.

Not only does the size of the room make it more manageable, it is less expensive on materials also, so you can afford to indulge yourself in costly wallpapers, expensive ceramics or deep-pile carpets. A popular alternative to the fun theme is to decorate a cloakroom in traditional style with lots of polished wood, and old-fashioned fittings and accessories. Here a tiny handbasin, a roll of wallpaper and a pair of framed sepia photographs have successfully recreated a sense of timeless elegance at minimal cost in a downstairs cloakroom, once a coat cupboard.

You may find you can decorate such a room inexpensively with left-overs from other rooms, or end-of-line bargains, leaving extra in the budget for a specially designed compact cloakroom basin like this one; or space-saving, sliding shower doors and wall-hung storage. Check out the ranges before you buy as there are many pieces specifically designed for small spaces including corner basins, corner shower trays and folding doors.

This cloakroom may be modestly sized, but it's big on style. A strictly traditional theme, co-ordinating plenty of polished wood with an Edwardian-style striped paper and sporting prints, makes this multi-functional room unexpectedly warm and inviting.

Custom-made shower makes a style statement

If you are lucky enough to have the space and resources to install a custom-made shower like this one, you have a marvellous opportunity to build in all the features you really want for both practicality and style.

The scheme needn't be cool blue and chrome, of course: creams and golds with a touch of rich red would create a suitably opulent atmosphere. While traditional picture tiles, etched glass

Clean lines and cool colours are the appeal of this elegant wrap-around shower complex, perfect for the luxury bathroom or en suite to the master bedroom.

and a polished wood panel surround would instantly conjure up an old-fashioned feel. However, the latest look is sleek, streamlined and environmentally friendly: so team those modern units with plenty of natural materials, such as sisal, wood, baskets, shells and stones.

Personal convenience is the other big advantage with this made-to-measure feature. It is obviously designed for those with busy lifestyles rather than to encourage relaxation and meditation, with a large walk-in shower cubicle used as the starting point for other smart, built-in features. These help integrate the shower more neatly into the rest of the room, as well as providing useful storage. Deep shelves both inside and around the enclosure offer a safe haven for bottles and jars, while towels are easily within reach on open shelves.

This fully-fitted shower cubicle fits perfectly into the corner of a large bedroom and is curtained off for greater privacy.

For those who prefer showers to baths, converting a spare bedroom or little-used living area into a luxury shower room is an attractive option, particularly if it can be combined with a variety of exercise equipment to create your own home gym. Some feel strongly enough to find the space by doing away with a bath altogether and replacing it with a shower, and this is an option worth considering if your bathroom really is the wrong size and shape to make a bath worthwhile.

Shower cubicles — good use of small spaces

Since a shower takes up remarkably little space — it need only be the size of the smallest shower tray — you can fit one into virtually any spare cupboard or corner of a room to provide extra walk-in facilities. It could usefully ease the burden on a busy bathroom and be a boon for larger households with no other scope to expand.

By moving the immersion heater elsewhere, this former airing cupboard now provides the perfect place for a luxury walk-in shower off the main bathroom. Wood-effect panelling has created that sleek, built-in look with carefully chosen wood and pottery accessories to complete the natural/neutral scheme of the main room with its sisal matting floor.

Cubicle doors are available in a standard range of sizes and fin-

A walk-in shower may be fitted neatly into any odd corner, at the end of a corridor, even in a redundant cupboard large enough to fit a base tray, to provide a smart and very useful addition to the main bathroom.

ishes to suit most locations; simply buy the sections that suit your needs, with chrome, gold or white finish and clear, smoked, bronzed or even Victorian-style etched glass. Doors may open out-wards if you have the room; alternatively, choose a sliding or fold-ing style where space is limited. The inside needs to be completely waterproof, so paint, tile or panel to complement other decorations. Note the effect of the neutral mauve-gray tiles lining the cubicle opposite which subtly give the impression of the shower being much larger inside than it really is: a plain white or patterned style would never blend so well with its surroundings.

A shower cubicle can be fitted into a small alcove or built-in cupboard; a corner of the bedroom for ensuite facilities, even in the space under the stairs. Re-siting access into the area may be necessary and the positioning of the existing plumbing needs to be considered.

Remember that a fully enclosed shower cubicle requires some form of waterproof lighting switched from outside the area. Usually the light will be fitted out of reach on the wall or ceiling, and outdoor globes or bulkheads designed for garden use are both a practical and stylish solution. Always check with a qualified electrician that the fitting is safe.

The deep maroon of the tiles has been integrated with the rest of the decor by the clever use of a simple stencilled border design.

Hallways

First impressions are very important, and the first glimpse that many people have of your home is quite often the hall. It does not matter how hard you have planned and beautifully decorated your other rooms, if the linking areas leave a lot to be desired, the effect is never quite the same.

Because of the amount of traffic through a hallway, the decorative elements should be durable. Likewise, try to ensure you have the maximum amount of light. If this is at a minimum, consider opening up doorways into rooms that have natural light available. Artificial lighting lacks character, so highlight areas of interest, such as bookshelves, the stairwell, or a seating area.

Hallways, by their very nature, normally contain many interesting angles and shapes, so use these to your advantage to create an interesting space within your home.

Narrow hallways should be decorated with caution. The white here maximizes the illusion of space and the warm colours in the painting on the far wall make the hall appear shorter as the wall advances rather than recedes. Position pictures on one side wall only or the room will appear even narrower.

BELOW: A large hallway, like this one, can be turned into a lobby area with the addition of a comfortable chair and sideboard.

LEFT: Lighting should be used to highlight areas within the hallway, such as the stairwell featured here. All too often they can appear dark and claustrophobic.

All the colours of spice for warmth and softness

N eutrals are always easy to live with, and the warmer tones especially so. This wonderfully classical hallway is simple in its styling. The arched windows are a major feature and the chosen curtain style accentuates their shape. The use of sheers allows for maximum light to flood into the house and the knotted and draped swags add a little colour and interest. Never attempt to hang straight top curtains on arched windows as they won't hang correctly and the finished look will be messy. For the best

The use of warm neutrals and carefully chosen fabrics ensures a light, classically styled stairway.

and neatest end result, curtains for windows like this should be carefully cut out around a template of the arch from which they are to hang.

The caramel-coloured carpet is a deep enough tone to be practical without appearing heavy. The walls are also decorated in a neutral shade and with a soft sandstone blockwork effect. This can be achieved by either using a paint finish or by hanging a faux effect wallpaper of the same design.

To add tonal variety to the room, the wooden staircase and window frame have been painted in a matt white. This also makes the walls and carpet appear richer. The top of the newel post has been marbled to add subtle interest.

Once again, it is the accessories that enhance the feel of the finished room by providing deeper, richer tones within the neutral colour scheme. The terracotta urns, small busts and bowls have been grouped together to add depth and considerable style to the windowsill. In addition, the golden velvet and brocade cushions at the other end of the sill are positioned to create a seating area from which to view the outside world.

Decorative items like these always have a stronger effect on a room when grouped together. If the terracotta items had been spaced along the window, for example, they would definitely have lost a considerable amount of their impact.

Natural cotton and jute accessories look good in either a classical or contemporary setting. Their neutral tones don't jar and their texture is endlessly satisfying.

Spicy and natural colours – especially when combined in subtly patterned wallpapers like the marble-effect one here – work very well with plain sheer fabrics, as the subtle colours don't overwhelm the fine quality.

Neutrals and checks create a rural feel

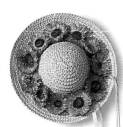

Country accessories are very important to the finished look of a hallway. Flower arrangements like these would make a perfect accent for, say, a blue or green hallway.

This country hall has also been decorated using paint. It may have this in common with the hall featured on the previous page, but due to the type of colours chosen, the look really is quite dramatically different.

Here, the colours are taken from the warm side of the colour wheel, creating an inviting atmosphere for the entrance to a house. As this is an area with plenty of headroom and open spaces, these colours are the perfect option as they visually draw in the walls and ceiling, making a room look more inviting.

A natural floor matting has been used to add a mellow texture to the floor and it continues up the staircase. The mahogany turned hand rail and spindles contrast well with both the walls and floor, toning in with the chosen colour scheme. This wood finish is also echoed in both the curtain pole and the wall-mounted clock positioned halfway up the stairs. The area under the stairs has been painted to blend with the walls.

To create a certain style, you need to enlist the help of some

Red and orange are warm colours that introduce a welcoming and cosy feel to a room. Different patterns can work well together as long as they are based on the same colours.

elements that have a particularly evocative feel and enormous fun can be had searching out the perfect accessories. Here, an informal element has been added through the ultimate in country fabric design, the red and white check fabrics. These

Check fabrics in traditional colours are always successful in a setting like this one as the colours are bold but the pattern not too overwhelming.

particular curtains sweep onto the floor which is especially practical when hanging over a front or back door as it helps to keep draughts at bay.

The pieces of occasional furniture and accessories have a rustic appearance and work well in the finished room as they offset the red, contrasting accent colour. The chair by the hall table has been incorporated into its setting by adding a cushion made of red and white checks, but this time a small gingham fabric has been used rather than the larger squares of the curtains. The scale is just perfect.

Studio rooms and bedsits

With space increasingly at a premium, more and more people are converting bedrooms into places where one can study and relax, as well as sleep.

This is a great example of a multifunctional bedroom. In fact, it is hard to tell if it has been designed foremost as a sleeping area or a sitting room. The Moroccan theme has such an impact on the room its function seems unimportant; primarily it is a place where you would want to spend plenty of time.

This atmospheric bedroom doubles as a stylish sitting room. Situated at the top of the house, the room has a sloping ceiling and the area under the eaves has been used cleverly to house a low-level bed, which also doubles as an additional seating area. Both ceiling and walls have been colourwashed in a soft blue to add to the height of the space and to soften the angular walls.

Many people would say that a plaster pink or terracotta wall would be more in keeping with the Moroccan colour scheme. However, in this case, the room has benefited from a colour that recedes rather than an advancing warm colour which naturally draws in a room. Instead of the walls, the mellow wooden floor and jewel-coloured soft furnishings provide the Mediterranean-style warmth the scheme needs.

As with any themed room, the accessories set the tone, and here are some ideal examples. Moroccan, low-level, hard-wood tables and traditional lanterns add atmosphere but they also help to keep the detailing low within the room. This draws attention away from the relatively low ceilings, making them appear rather less oppressive.

Hand-painted tiles have been used to create a border around the door frame. Ceramic tiles are used to decorate all rooms in a traditional Moroccan home, so they look perfect here and are proof that they need not only be used in a kitchen.

A Moroccan-style scheme should include a few key elements, such as strong jewel colours reminiscent of the heat of the Mediterranean; fabrics embossed with gold or featuring Arabic motifs; "magic" carpets, and accessories in ornately carved dark timber and burnished copper. Here, the elements sit together easily, creating a relaxed room that works equally well for either of its uses.

It is sometimes difficult to obtain accessories that are exact to the period or style of a room. But quite often an item in a style that is complementary to the room adds personality to the finished scheme. These novel "crown" mirrors are a good example.

Moroccan-style tiles can add interest to any room whose decor is based on this theme. There are a number of suppliers, so hunt around for the design you like the most.

Sophisticated graphite and steel for a loft room

If your home benefits from having high ceilings, as is so often the case in a studio flat or loft, it gives you the opportunity of creating a two-tier layout for your room. By raising elements off the ground, additional floor space is freed up in the room, giving a larger working area. This is the perfect way of adding scope to a room that could be used for more than one purpose.

This room has benefitted from a design approach just like this, as the bed has been raised on a sturdy metal structure. Many contemporary interior designers like to use this style of semi-industrial furniture, as it has clean, simple lines and is very functional. In this room, both the bed frame and the simple metal staircase have been finished in a matt metallic paint, which works extremely well within the monochromatic colour scheme.

Many monochrome schemes can appear hard but this room has a softness derived from the mellow tones of the bleached timber flooring. In fact, when you look more closely at the room you can see that it is made up of many tones ranging from the hard black desk, chair and filing cabinet, through to the soft flooring and finally the walls. It is this variation of tone that gives dimension to the room. Think of the room as it would appear in a black and white photograph; if there was no variation

Tubular steel and chrome furniture is perfect to complement a room such as the one shown here.

If you are unable to afford furniture with a modern-style finish such as graphite and steel, try one of the spray paint finishes available in DIY stores.

of tone, the room would look flat and uninteresting. As it is, the tonal variety adds dimension and depth to the space.

Each piece of furniture in the room has been chosen for its metallic quality and smooth lines. They each complement the semi-industrial bed structure and continue the contemporary feel of the room. The bed has been dressed using a simple quilt cover in a bright yellow and grey: primary colours are often used to enliven a monochromatic colour scheme such as this one. To further redress the balance, a vase of yellow tulips creates a splash of colour to the right of the room.

Modern styling takes a much gentler approach than that of the 1980s. The grey bed frame and mellow tones of the floorboards are far more comfortable to live with than the starkly contrasting black and white which used to be combined so freely in the contemporary living space.

Storage solutions for one-room living

Storage assumes enormous importance in a one-room-living situation. Everything must earn its place if the space is to function efficiently and living is not to be uncomfortable. This is where practical planning comes into its own.

Here an entire storage wall for books, television, video, tapes, cassettes and CDs is used to create a room divider between the sitting and sleeping space and the dining/kitchen area. Companion shelves on the reverse side are used to store glasses, china and everything needed for cooking and the table. Mirrors magnify the space and give increased light.

When storage like this is being planned, it is wise to measure the things you need to store (including assessing their weight) so you can ensure all shelves, cupboards and drawers are deep, tall, wide and strong enough to accommodate everything. This may mean having some adjustable shelves.

If you are faced with a typical "quart in a pint pot" situation, it may be wise to call in an expert in built-in furniture, or a carpenter, who can work to your specifications and tailor-make storage to your requirements. Alternatively, you could adapt ready-made storage yourself, perhaps incorporating adjustable shelves on wall-mounted slots, or metal scaffold-type or industrial shelving if you plan a hi-tech look.

The storage can be painted — as here — so it is unobtrusive and fades into the background. Alternatively, you could paint it to

Shiny, reflective surfaces create a sense of spaciousness. Use mirrors wherever possible and lay a glossy floorcovering, such as vinyl or polished wood veneer.

Although basically just a "bed sitting room", this living area has been given a touch of class by using traditional furniture and furnishings set in a sophisticated cream colour scheme.

contrast and stand out. This would work well in a hi-tech space, or if you wanted to unify disparate pieces.

The mainly neutral colour scheme in this studio creates a tranquil atmosphere which helps to increase the apparent space, leading to an uncluttered look. There is a good textural mix – the blonde wood floor is softened by a large rug (which helps to divide the area into zones), and the bed has a practical fringed throw-over cover. The large potted plant adds extra visual detailing and casts interesting shadows onto the wall and ceiling under artificial lighting conditions.

Creating a room within a room

To live successfully in a small space, you need to make the most of every nook and cranny. Of course, if you are lucky enough to have a tall room, then there is the opportunity to move upwards as well as across the floor space, which is precisely what has been achieved here.

Making a room within a room is most frequently attained by the careful positioning of the furniture or by creating a division — either hard or soft. In this studio room, however, a bedroom has been made by building a raised area at one end of the room.

Minimal living can only really be achieved if you have the storage space to accompany it. Here, large cupboards are incorporated into the raised platform sleeping area.

Cupboards are incorporated into the structure, thereby cleverly solving the other problem attached to small-space living — where to store everything.

To maximize space, as much clutter as possible should be ejected from the home, or at least stored away. Although creating storage areas might initially seem like a waste of valuable space, ultimately it is well worth it as it makes everyday living a great deal less cluttered and more straightforward.

The best way to create the illusion of space is to decorate the room in simple, pale colours. Don't draw in the walls or ceiling with dark reds, blues or greens, as this will only serve to make the place seem more claustrophobic. The fresh white paint on all the surfaces in this room make it a crisp, clean area. The walls recede because they are not broken up with dominating pictures, or interrupted by shelves of knick-knacks.

The few pieces of furniture are black, chosen to contrast stylishly with the white background. The gun-metal grey carpet is equally plain and smart, and it unifies the decor of the room exremely successfully.

Too much black and white might become difficult to live with, so the sleeping area at the top of the metal step ladder is softened with tungsten lighting, which gives off a warm yellow glow. This softening effect is further enhanced by the pastel shades used for the bedding.

Never forget the strong statement that can be made by using all white with a touch of black or grey. Or follow a monochromatic theme with just these three colours. Accents can be provided by natural wood, terracotta or green plants.

FOCUS FILE

You will now be very familiar with a variety of styles of room, and if you are planning to completely renovate, or even just redecorate the rooms in your home you have hopefully come a long way towards making a decision about the style you would like. The rooms featured in the Style File chapter on pages 26-141 will have given you a wide range of ideas and you will be able to determine why these rooms work so successfully, but there is still a large amount of information to help you make wise choices when selecting the principal elements that will make up your dream home. Over the following pages, we examine the various peripheral products on the market from which you can make these all-important choices.

We look at the types of flooring and wallcoverings that are most suitable for each room — those that withstand stains, steam, condensation and grease, depending on whether they are for the kitchen or bathroom. Floors take a great deal of wear and tear, so some background information on what is available will help you make the right decision. Technology has played a large role in developing materials that are ideal for the kitchen or bathroom environments, having the beauty of traditional materials but the durability only space-age science can produce. We also look at floorings that are attractive yet hardwearing for living rooms.

In the section on window treatments we examine everything from the simplest blind to the most elaborate of drapes. This will enable you to choose the treatment that will best suit not only the style of window, but the rest of the room decor, too.

Our section on fabrics opens with some extremely handy hints on how colour works in relation to design and texture. We then consider choices of fabrics for myriad rooms and furnishings. Finally, we look at the ever-pressing problems of lighting and storage – and come up with an amazing variety of solutions for every room in your home.

A wooden dado panel, treated with a good varnish sealant, is an efficient way of protecting bathroom walls from splashed water but it does not have to be dull, as this exuberant treatment demonstrates.

Walls and floors

These are the largest areas to decorate or cover and so will be the most dominant within your scheme, despite the fact that they are "broken up" by other elements: walls are interrupted by windows, fireplaces and doors; floors by the furniture.

Before you begin, remember to relate the size of any pattern and depth of colour to the scale of the surface on which they are to be used. Bold designs and strong colours work well on large floors and walls, and next to big windows; paler colours and less flamboyant patterns look better on smaller areas.

Aim to plan your scheme as professionally as possible and this means working from the floor up. The interior designer always tries to start with the flooring and works the scheme for the rest of the room around this, partly because a floor covering should last well through several different changes of decor, and if you choose wisely, through at least two or three generations.

When it comes to living rooms, many people don't think beyond a fitted carpet, but this is not always a sensible option as a carpet in a dining area can become grubby fairly quickly, and areas in front of a sofa or favourite chair can be scuffed by television watchers. Instead, consider laying a hard, resilient or smooth flooring (wool, tiles, linoleum or vinyl) and use rugs to soften the seating areas.

If you do select a carpet, choose the very best you can afford. This means considering the fibre used in manufacture (an 80:20 wool and nylon mix is a good choice); the method of making; the type of pile and number of tufts per square centimetre/inch. A

looped or close-cut velvet pile is more practical in areas of heavy wear; longer piles will flatten in use.

Make sure you choose a practical colour. Mid-tones are better than pastels or very dark colours, as both show up marks. Bold patterns can look as though they are rising up at you, so a muted colour and textured or mini-print design might be a better choice.

Natural floor coverings are also available (such as sisal, rush, and seagrass mattings, jute and coirs) with attractive, heavily-textured surfaces, which are popular for living rooms. Although not as soft underfoot as carpet, they are extremely hardwearing. However, they can be difficult to keep pristine as stains may become ingrained and dried food spills will need picking out with a blunt knife!

The wall treatment in your living room will very much depend on the style of the room and whether you want to enhance its original architectural character or whether you prefer to superimpose a particular look on a rather bland room.

Floral patterned wall coverings in soft, faded colours will suggest a country cottage image; a stronger, flowing floral pattern, hung above a painted Anaglypta-covered dado rail gives a Victorian Arts and Crafts flavour; classical images in clear colours, on the other hand, can create the Neo-classical look of a grand country house.

The primary requirements of a bathroom floor

A boldly coloured carpet provides the focus in this modern setting, while the striped cushions and piano stool cover echo the pattern of the wood flooring.

The subdued flooring contrasts with a riot of wall colour provided by friezes and a pop-art painting. Note the second painting resting against the wall gallery-style, as if waiting to be hung.

covering are that it should be waterproof and easy to clean. Treated wooden flooring, ceramic glazed tiles and linoleum all meet these criteria, whereas natural woven coir or sisal, though popular, are not so practical. They retain moisture and can give off a damp odour. Carpets need to be of a water-repellant material, specially designed for bathrooms. Rugs should be washable and with a non-slip backing if used on a shiny surface.

Walls also need to be resistant to prolonged exposure to steam and to splashed water around the fixtures. Tiles are a perfect solution, providing the necessary impermeability with a wide choice of colour and pattern.

This natural maple floor echoes the warmth of the terracotta walls as well as being water-resistant and washable.

Combining white with delicately patterned, blue spotted tiles to cover the whole of the wall surface makes this small bathroom practical, light and pretty.

Kitchens can benefit from both painted walls and floors. Use water-based paints on all surfaces to make colour matching easier. In such cases, protect the woodwork with a coat or two of acrylic varnish. This is worthwhile for a distressed paint finish on, say, furniture or skirting boards.

Many colour schemes include stained and painted timber — either natural tones or more colourful washes — for both walls and floors. And with a quality varnish and sealant over the top, most timbers can now be used in areas such as the sink without danger of warping or distortion. Ceramic, marble and quarry tiles also offer a very versatile and practical finish for both walls and floors in a kitchen.

A painted surface needs to be wipeable as does a wallpaper covering, which should also be water-resistant. Wallpapers designed for bathrooms are made of vinyl with a polymer coating. An alternative solution to meeting the dual requirements is to have two types of wall-covering: one for areas which will get wet and one for the rest of the wall space. Small areas of tiles make perfect splashbacks for a bath or washbasin and can be made into a decorative feature in themselves, they are also the most practical solution for a shower cubicle.

A larger design feature also meeting the need for protection against localized areas of water splashing and general humidity is to fit dado panelling to half-way up the walls and to paint or wall-paper the rest.

In the bathroom shown the painted walls are set off against a cream tongued-and-grooved dado which extends just beyond the

basin and the two are separated by a highly practical shelf. The natural woven matting on the floor is protected in front of the basin by a blue and white striped rug. The colours and informal geometry of the rug have been repeated in the che-querboard design painted

These roughly set tiles in earthy colours make a clever feature of the practical necessity of a splashback.

on the walls: a decorative effect requiring care and attention but perfectly feasible over a small area such as this and producing a highly individual, coordinated design.

The relatively small surface area of the walls in a bathroom lends itself to special decorative techniques, such as stencilling. Here a simple fleur-de-lys motif has been used to break up the expanse of tongue-and-groove panelling.

The cream tongued-and-grooved dado panel provides both a practical wall surface as well as a decorative feature. It is finished off with a shelf running all round the room to take all the necessities of a bathroom.

Here, paint finishes have been used to decorate both walls and floor. The timber floor has been painted and stencilled, while a more fanciful stencil has been applied to the plain white walls. A metallic paint effect gives the splashbacks and kitchen units added interest.

Ceramic tiles are particularly varied and can be laid in patterns of your own choice. Consider combining different colours of the same hand-painted motif, using moulded dado rails, or insetting picture tiles among plain white tiles. If you are planning on using tiles as a splashback, take advantage of the modern adhesives and grouts now available as they team with the product to create a bacteria-free and hard-wearing surface.

For the kitchen floor, in addition to ceramic tiles, there is also a wonderful selection of slate, terracotta and stone, all of which are extremely hard-wearing. These products have a unique quality and style, but will need more maintenance than other types of hard flooring if they are to avoid greasy stains becoming permanent. They are also expensive options, will definitely need laying by an expert, are hard underfoot, and any dropped dishes will undoubtedly break on such a surface, so bear these points in mind when making your choice.

Softer floorings include natural timber, cork tiles and vinyl which together offer an extensive palette of colours and designs for your kitchen. If you are laying cork or vinyl, it is best to prepare the bare floor first by laying small sheets of hardboard. Soak the boards first and lay them rough side up, securing them with ring nails. These have more grip than ordinary nails and will prevent the floor surface from shifting later on.

Cushion vinyl is a cheaper and warmer alternative to hard tiles and there are many very passable imitations available both as tiles and sheet flooring. The disadvantage of using timber or vinyl is the fact that water can penetrate to the floor below. So if any of your appliances were to overflow or leak, you could end up with problems. You should therefore choose these types of product with care.

Ceramic tiles now incorporate every style and theme of decorating imaginable. This little badger would bring a smile to your face on the busiest of days.

Small insets between larger floor tiles break up a surface and give it added interest.

Window treatments

The style of window treatment you choose should depend not only upon the shape and style of the window concerned, but also on the room's style and size. Each room of the house will have different factors, such as light and ventilation, to be taken into consideration as well.

An additional requirement for a bathroom window is that it should maintain privacy, unless the room is not overlooked. Frosted glass with a ventilation fan is functional and inexpensive but can be rather clinical. So soften the look with some kind of fabric curtain. Using sheer white fabrics, such as muslin or lace, is a good solution, since they still allow plenty of light through and

A simple Roman blind makes an effective but unobtrusive window treament.

Elegant, practical, flexible: the Venetian blind finds its ideal place in the bathroom.

add a pretty, feminine touch. Alternatively, since the curtains over frosted glass do not need to be drawn, this gives a perfect opportunity for interesting decorative treatments, such as swags and tails or a single full-length curtain with a fixed heading, drawn into a matching tieback.

Bathroom windows are usually quite small, so elaborate fabric treatments for the short curtains are generally not appropriate. Too much fabric will also encourage mildew in the folds. Choose plain or small patterned fabrics and simple heading treatments, such as tab tops or pencil heading tape. Roman or roller blinds

This frosted glass is prevented from looking too cold and functional by the bold Roman blind and pelmet in fabric to match the wallpaper.

Sheer fabrics can be used as a contrast to the hard surface of a frosted glass window without reducing the amount of light.

The swags and tails on this window covering have been created by cleverly draping a length of fabric around a heavy wooden pole. But do bear in mind the expense of such treatments – the amount of fabric required is considerable.

are practical and effective treatments.

Venetian blinds are particularly suitable: they come in a good range of styles and colours. Wooden or metal-slatted shutters fulfil the same function as blinds but require slightly more complicated fittting.

When it comes to choosing fabrics that are suitable for window treatments in a living room, bear in mind how much wear and tear the curtains will be subjected to. For large windows, it is worth investing in an automatic drawing system operated by cords (either worked by hand or electrically), which saves pulling – and therefore soiling – the curtains' leading edges.

The style of the treatment should relate to the architectural period of the room and the overall decorating theme. Conventionally, main living or dining room curtains reach to the floor, but although this is undoubtably more elegant, it is not always practical if there is a radiator or window seat under the window, for example. Sill-length curtains are a compromise in such a case.

Curtain fabrics can also provide an opportunity to bring in some contrasting colour accents to enliven the overall scheme, or to provide a balance between patterned and plain surfaces. For example, cushions on a modern, square sofa, upholstered in a plain fabric could include large, circular, geometric-patterned cushions, as well as conventional bolsters covered in a smart tartan check, and some square and triangular ones in plain, but interestingly textured, fabric that matches the curtains.

On elaborately dressed windows, you may prefer to have a blind under the drapes to serve as the means of keeping out the night, rather than drawing the curtains each evening. Even if not

A light, transparent fabric that allows sunlight to filter through is perfect for a south-facing room as the curtains can be drawn by day to create a cool atmosphere.

practical, a simple roller or Roman blind used in conjunction with curtains, can be a most effective treatment in the living room.

The secret to successful kitchen window treatments lies in simplicity. Because kitchen curtains need more regular laundering than those in any other room in the home they should be simple to remove, re-attach and dress, and preferably be made from easily washable fabrics. Be aware, however, that most lined curtains should, where possible, be dry cleaned as even if the main fabric is washable, the linings may shrink.

Roman blinds are one simple option in a kitchen. There is very little fabric to trap dust and grime and they can be made in almost

Simple, unlined curtains such as these can be quickly removed and laundered – a necessity in a steamy kitchen. Ties that are in a contrasting fabric – rather than more formal hooks – are used to hang the curtains on the pole.

If your kitchen has a private outlook you may decide not to use a curtain or blind and opt for a simple drape of fabric that frames the window instead. To achieve this effect, buy metal "spiral" holders which enable you to wind the fabric into attractive knots at each top corner.

any fabric, and create an impact on the design of a room. They are also very simple to operate and are easily drawn up when not in use, making them less likely to get in the way of wall-mounted units or sink and cooker areas.

If you are the sort of person who tires of things easily, then a drape made of a simple square of fabric the size of your window recess will offer you the option of change. As you can see here, the same square has been attached to a window frame using ornate metal hooks, and it can be drawn up into a blind with two simple ties. The same drape can also be drawn to one side of the window to create a curtain using a tie.

Of course, fabric window treatments are not the only option. Wooden shutters and various forms of blind are also available — everything from the metal or timber Venetian blind to the simple rafia roller. Stained glass or shelves set into the window recess are alternative ways of creating privacy in a decorative manner.

This square of fabric is made from an unlined, large check cotton fabric, which has been framed with a border of the same fabric cut on the cross. It can easily be drawn to one side of the window and fastened with a tie.

Fabrics and soft furnishings

Choosing the soft furnishings – and this includes the furniture upholstery, loose covers, curtains, blinds, cushions and bolsters – for any room, is often one of the most enjoyable parts of decorating, as at this stage, the hard work of painting and papering is probably complete. However, some of us may find we need to decorate a room around an existing patterned sofa or we might fall in love with a range of bedding and need to design a room around that. If you are in this situation, you can quite often benefit from the expertise of the person who designed that particular bedding or the fabric covering the sofa.

Designing around a patterned fabric can be simpler than you think as long as you take note of the proportions in which the designer has used the colours. In this instance, blue is followed by white and then yellow and pink in smaller quantities.

The designer will have spent a great deal of time trying different colours and shades together in their fabric, until the right effect was achieved. If you are planning to have this fabric in your home it means that you find the same blend of colours are also to your taste. So take advantage of it.

First look closely at the fabric and consider the proportions in which the colours have been used. Then make a note of them, the greatest first. Take the fabric on the bed featured here, for example. The background colour, blue, is the predominant colour in the design, followed by the white, and then the yellow and pink in almost equal quantities.

Now consider your room. What element will take the largest block of colour? In the case of this bedroom, it was the walls, followed by the impressive ceiling, and then the floor. Always remember to think of the room when it is full of furniture; the floor area may equal the ceiling area when the room is empty, but this changes with the addition of the bed. Make a note of this information, and decorate the room with colour in the same proportions as used in the fabric.

So, to complement this fabric, the room has been decorated with the main block of blue on the walls, the white on the ceiling (the next largest area), and then the pink and yellow in smaller quantities. Mellow yellow tones were introduced in the wood on the floor, and in splashes of a purer yellow on the bed

Fabric designers spend a lot of time working out a good balance of colour. So when a large expanse of fabric dominates, such as a bedcover or sofa, you can be guided by this to decorate the rest of the room.

valance and as a border. Finally, the pink colour was used as an all-important accent on the cushion on the chair and, to add balance, the pink carnations in the vase on the side table.

If you have already decorated your room and still need to choose your soft furnishings, there are a number of considerations to bear in mind. Remember, it is the fabrics and soft furnishings that make a house into a home.

In the living room, the upholstery, cushions, covers, window treatments and small accessories will help to create a cosy

For luxurious seating, fill a sofa with a myriad of cushions. The throw arranged beneath this pile cleverly disguises a particularly old piece of upholstery.

ambience, and give the owner a chance to imprint their personality on the scheme. First, when deciding on upholstery, practical
aspects have to be considered – what sort of wear and tear will
the furniture receive?

For main living areas, and this includes dining rooms and large
family kitchens, who are the chief inhabitants? For young children
and rumbustious teenagers, loose covers in a sensible colour and
hardwearing, easy-to-clean fabrics are usually a wise option. If the
room is used mainly by adults, however, then paler colours, tight
and more fragile fabrics could be chosen. But bear in mind that
most seating does take a fair amount of punishment, so very pale
colours and delicate textures are best avoided.

It is wise to consider some form of stain protection for the main
items of soft furnishings in your living room. Also, always check on
the quality of fillings, and the fire retardancy of the upholstery and
fabrics, to ensure they conform to fire regulations.

Above all, the upholstered furniture should be comfortable for
everybody who is going to sit and relax in the living room. Some
people like to sprawl in a softly upholstered sofa or chair, while
others prefer a more upright position, with seating which is firmer
to sit on, with good support for the head.

When deciding on fabrics, aim to achieve a good balance
between pattern and plain, and always remember to relate the
size of any design and the strength of colour to the scale of the
surface on which it is to appear.

Use large, flowing florals on well-rounded chairs and sofas;

*Cushion covers are the
perfect way to inject instant
colour and variation of
pattern into a living room. If
you are using lots of
different patterns, tie them
together by drawing on a
narrow range of colours.*

*Plump cushions and an
upholstered window seat fill
this ornate bay window.
Austrian blinds complete the
formal look.*

checks, stripes and geometrics on square or rectangular stream-lined pieces; neat mini-prints and checks on small stools or dining chairs. The same rule applies to fabric for curtains and blinds. Plain fabrics are a wise choice for buttoned upholstery and curtains with very decorative headings as the treatment looks more spectacular.

Fabrics will also be used for occasional and dining table covers and napery, as well as for cushions and throws. Again, think of the practical apsects and choose fabrics that are easy to clean or launder if they are to be in a much-used situation.

It is also worth considering the source of your fabrics. Antique materials can often be bought quite inexpensively in markets or sales and — with the addition of some beading, braid or fringing — can be turned into wonderful tablecovers, cushions, or easy-to-make tie-up blinds.

When it comes to dressing a bed, the overall cover and bed linen are prominent players in the room's decoration. Many people find the comfort and convenience offered by quilts and pillow sets are the perfect solution to bedding options and they are now available in every style and colour imagin-able. Classic colours and styles work well for traditional bed-rooms, and brighter, bolder prints look better in more

Remember that the texture of your chosen upholstery fabric will affect the final colour. Velvets, plain jacquard weaves or brocades will provide a denser colour than say a glazed chintz or cotton/linen blend.

A traditional four-poster frame has been given the contemporary treatment here, with its simple and soft drapes of sheer fabric.

contemporary settings or children's rooms. However, remember that monochromatic schemes using neutral colours can create a very tranquil environment, whatever the style of the room, and this is worth considering, especially for when you are unwell or resting.

As bed linen is frequently laundered, easy-care cottons and polycottons are a bonus, but you might want to try traditional linens in a formal room. A bedspread, quilt or comforter can be in any fabric, but bear in mind that lighter colours will soil quicker than darker ones, whether from spilt coffee, animals or children.

For the more ambitious, think about embellishing the bed with drapes, curtains, pelmets and canopies. Bed drapes and canopies were historically used not purely for their aesthetic qualities; four posters, for example, were introduced with their heavily draped curtains designed to be drawn and close out the cold night air. Mosquito nets, which can be seen in many a contemporary bedroom scheme, were purely practical. It is only in recent years that we have recognised the softness and attention they can bring to the simplest of beds.

For those looking to create something beyond the standard divan, you can buy or make, or have made one of the following. The four-poster is a frame that surrounds the bed with, as the name suggests, four vertical posts supporting a top frame from which curtains or drapes can be hung. A half-tester, however, purely frames the headboard and pillowed area of the bed and it is either an integral part of the headboard or can be attached to the wall behind and above the bed. It consists of a back curtain, a pair of side curtains, and either a carved wooden or decorative metal pelmet or fabric valance. The curtains and fabric valance are attached to a wooden pelmet board that is about 15 cm (6 in) wider than the bed and can protrude up to 66 cm (26 in).

Bed drapes, as the name suggests, are pieces of fabric draped

Cushion pads are made in all manner of shapes and sizes. Here, round and rectangular are combined to emphasize the geometric shape of this sofa.

The bed need not be the main supply of pattern to the room. Indeed, a plain bed can look striking in a heavily decorated room.

A blanket or throw adds extra colour and pattern to a room while offering additional warmth to the bed if needed.

around, above or behind the bed. Drapes wrapped around a four-poster frame and down its vertical posts can look very contemporary, while a piece of fabric drawn up to create swags suspended from ornate gilt cherubs can add a truly decorative detail to a traditional room. You could also consider a corona — a frame from which curtains hang. A corona is normally semi-circular and is positioned centrally above the bed, and the curtains that hang from the corona then draw back to either side of the bed or headboard. A corona can be made from a simple, semi-circular pelmet board with curtains or a valance attached to the front edge, or be more ornate, and manufactured from carved timber or metal work.

This simple bed drape has been suspended from little gilt cherubs. It is very effective and quick to create.

This bed canopy has been suspended from two iron poles attached via chains from the ceiling. The fabric is threaded onto the poles through two channels sewn in the fabric.

But whatever atmosphere you hope to create in your bedroom, the soft furnishings will play a very important part in creating that finished look.

It is important that the designs and colours chosen are compatible with the colour scheme, but it is also important to ensure that the styles used are practical and functional. Bedding is laundered regularly and should be of a quality and fabric to allow this to happen successfully.

To create a simple canopy, suspend a ready-made wrought iron hoop on a chain from the ceiling above the centre of your bed. Then tie lengths of mosquito net onto the hoop. Alternatively, you could use a painted canopy as a practical and artistic alternative to fabric.

Don't feel that you need to rely on fabric to dress the area around a bed. The mural is also a clever way to draw attention towards a focal point in a bedroom. This form offers endless possibilities for any room from a style and pattern perspective, and has the added bonus of never needing to be taken down and laundered.

Take the room measurements with you when you shop (as well as colour samples of any existing items like the carpet), since there is no point in deciding on a large four-

seater sofa, only to find that it won't fit into the space that you have allowed for it.

Don't worry about choosing different pieces — you can always unify them by using the same fabric to cover all the items (most manufacturers and suppliers run a cover-in-customers' own-fabric service), or use a coordinated range of fabrics to mix-and-match curtains, covers and cushions. This is when a combination of plain and patterned fabrics come into their own. Use stripes or checks as a neutral link, and add contrast piping and trimmings

This wrought-iron four poster frame has been dressed simply using lengths of white voile. The fabric is attached to the frame with ties, and cream and white roses add decorative details on the inner corners.

in the same colour palette to unify and define the shape of the furniture.

In the living room, the sofa is arguably the most important piece of furniture. A well-dressed sofa can include an array of patterns and fabrics – the more the merrier – so long as you stick to the basic principles of the rules of colour.

If the window in your living room is architecturally outstanding, and you would like to draw attention to it (and it does not have to be covered), throw a sheer fabric such as muslin, voile or lace over a pole, positioned well above the top of the window.

Many people choose to decorate their room around a favoured set of bedding and curtaining. However, to create a more individual style of room, consider a more decorative style of window treatment such as this one.

The corner of a room can be the perfect place for this style of bed draping.

An unusual form of bed draperie has been created with a mural – something the more artistic may like to consider.

Kitchens and bathrooms, by their very nature, do not present quite so many opportunities for soft furnishings, with the exception of window treatments (already discussed on pages 152-157). However, larger kitchens will probably have a table and even if you do not want to cover it with a cloth you might like to provide seat (squab) cushions for the chairs. For nostalgic styles of kitchen (and bathroom storage), run up simple curtains which can be suspended on curtaln wires to cover gaps in units or underneath basins to camouflage unsightly pipework.

Lighting

Most designers spend a great deal of time considering the correct combination of lighting for each room in the home. However, I suspect that the kitchen is the one room where most people would instinctively consider mixing different types of lighting.

Common sense dictates that a kitchen should never be lit solely by a single central light as it will cast a shadow onto working areas and will not provide sufficient illumination. Many kitchens have a combination of central and under-unit concealed lighting, which is usually quite sufficient.

Fluorescent lighting has been used in domestic kitchens for many years. It is energy-efficient and gives out very little heat. However, the strips can sometimes emit a buzz and the light produced is very harsh and must be covered by a shade or shielded from the eye — it can cause damage if you look directly into its light. Fluorescent bulbs are also expensive to dim as they require additional connections to achieve this.

Halogen lighting has become increasingly popular. It takes its name from the fact that it is filled with halogen gas, enabling the bulb to reach very high temperatures which creates a very white light. This is part of the attraction as halogen lights produce true colours which do not distort.

Halogen spot- and recess lights are very small and unobtrusive, ideal for use with other forms of lighting. The bulbs are available in various strengths and widths of beam. This means you can use one bulb to create a wash of light while another can add a direct

This contemporary kitchen is enhanced by modern halogen light fittings, which offer peaks of directional lighting.

shaft of light using a narrow width of beam. In the kitchen, it is practical to install light switches at elbow height so they can easily be flicked on or off if your hands are full. Two-way switches are also essential if you have both an outside and inside door, and in rooms where there are two entrances, such as hallways and staircases.

In the bedroom, a reasonable quality of light is needed throughout. The lighting should encourage a calm and restful atmosphere, conducive to relaxation. At bedtime, the lighting should focus on the bed alone, making the remaining space less obtrusive and the bedroom appear more intimate and cosy. Recessed spot lights in the ceiling and side lights positioned at the bedside appear to be the ideal compromise as spots give an even light across the room — required for dressing, for example — and they can be attached to a dimmer switch

There are many styles of light switch now available, but this particular one is definitely the most discreet. It would look good in either a traditional or a contemporary bedroom setting.

to give the option of varying the intensity. Bedside lights offer soft reading light and are easily controlled once in bed.

Spotlights can also be purchased with a narrow beam, enabling features or accessories to be highlighted, for example, the bed as well as a fireplace or favourite painting. But always consider the balance of the room – lighting acts as an accent and is very powerful, so it can make a room look one-sided and out of proportion.

Other types of lighting that you could consider include recessed spot lights, uplighters, downlighters, and lighting troughs,

This room has an even light in the day, but look at how the directional recessed spots have been positioned for night-time. This layout will highlight the bed, fireplace and the table displaying the Bonsai tree at the far side of the room.

to name a few. And, of course, there are also the more traditional side lights and pendants.

Think of the atmosphere you want to create, both in the day and at night. If your bedroom is multifunctional and you have a work area within the room, your lighting requirements will need to combine the practical with the aesthetic. For home studies, you will need to install the three main types of lighting: general, ambient and background.

As most living rooms serve several different purposes, the lighting needs to be as flexible as possible. Aim to have several different circuits, separately controlled, and to fix dimmer switches to one or two of them, to help you adjust the lighting for different moods. Have plenty of socket outlets for table and standard lamps to avoid the problem (and danger) or trailing flexes. Other fixed lighting, such as wall lights and pendants, will need to be positioned to light various surfaces clearly. It might well be worth your while making a scale plan of the room on some graph paper (see pages 9-10 for more details). This will help you to plot the position of all the lighting services accurately at the outset.

If the room has a second door or access to the garden, dual-switch the lights to operate from both points of entry.

Task lighting is necessary to illuminate a dining table without causing glare, to light any desk area, to enable you to see to read or sew, and to see inside units and cupboards. Accent or display lighting can be used to light a picture, wall-hanging or a floral

Now that halogen light is being used more and more, the style of fittings is becoming increasingly wide ranging. Here, frosted-glass sails and a fine metal mesh add a soft and original filter to the white light.

Chandeliers are the epitome of traditional elegance. Antique versions can be expensive, especially when re-wired for today's use. For a less costly option, buy reproduction, straight from the shelves of lighting departments or DIY stores.

display. It is also an attractive way of lighting a collection inside a glass-fronted cabinet, in an alcove or niche, or display shelves.

Light shining down or up through glass shelves is always effective. And don't underestimate the use of pelmet lighting to enhance a beautiful fabric or interesting window treatment.

When you are selecting light fittings or lamp shades, always see them lit as well as unlit first. This is because the effect can be totally different when the light shines through the fitting or shade, affecting the colour of the light and area of illumination.

Most fittings will be a permanent fixture, becoming part of the structure of the room. Others, like table lamps and standard

In a living room it is essential that you don't limit yourself to one form of lighting alone. Strive to use both functional and atmospheric lights.

lamps are reasonably portable, and are usually referred to as decorative lighting.

Whatever fittings you choose, they should be in sympathy with the architectural style of the room, and its decorations and furnishings. Eyeball spots in the ceiling, for example, may suit a hi-tech interior, but would look inappropriate in a period home or with a country cottage decor.

Finally, when lighting bathrooms think safety-first as water and electricity do not mix. Switches must be positioned outside the room or on pull cords. Shades should be ceiling fitted and sealed from damp. Consult a qualified electrician if in doubt.

The interesting shafts of light reflected in the metal splash backs are produced by short lengths of concealed strip lighting.

This is a good example of the effect that simple side lights can have on a room, highlighting the bed and casting shadow on the remaining space.

Storage solutions

When it comes to planning living room storage, you need to assess exactly which items you want to put away neatly – and which you might use as part of an attractive display on dressers, shelves, or inside glass-fronted cabinets. Take into consideration the size and weight of all the things you want to store. Large books, for example, cannot be housed in a flimsy, narrow-shelved bookcase.

Your lifestyle, the room's decor and its size and shape will all influence your choice of storage. In a room with projecting chimney breasts, for example, you can make maximum use of the two recesses for base units, or a desk with shelving above; or use them for display cabinets or an imposing bureau bookcase.

The wood or other finish that you select will also help you to enhance the style of the room. Pine shelving and other storage pieces will suit a country-style living room, but mahogany, yew, walnut or satinwood will add elegance to a more formal room. If your theme is modern, then a pale wood such as ash or sycamore, a contemporary paint finish, modern laminates, or industrial materials like rubber, steel, latex or chrome, would all be a stylish choice.

If none of these appeal, or are affordable, you could combine secondhand pieces with built-in cupboards, all painted to blend with the scheme. You might even try a decorative paint finish such as dragging, marbling or stencilling to unify the various items.

Most living rooms need storage space for a wide range of items, from CDs and video tapes to children's toys. In a dual-

purpose room, you may need to house even more items, such as computers and stationery — or even spare bedding if the room is a studio or the sofa is to be used for overnight guests.

Hide ugly hardware with elegant drapes hung from a decorative metal frame.

First of all, decide exactly what you want to put where, then measure everything. You could combine free- with tailor-made furniture or dress up some junk shop finds. Whichever option you choose, remember to take your tape measure with you when you go shopping, or make a careful note when commissioning a carpenter. You will then ensure that the insides of any storage unit are as practical as possible.

Glass shelving and modular wood cabinets provide ultra-modern display storage.

Many people make the mistake of thinking that the more cupboards you have in the kitchen, the better. While it may be true to
say that you can never have too many well-designed storage units,
efficient organization of the contents of your kitchen offers a
better solution. Cupboards need not only be at ground level, nor
need they all be of the same height. Units attached to walls at
eye-level height make good use of what can often be wasted
space. They are also especially useful for storing items that need
to be kept away from children's sticky fingers or, if you have glass-
fronted doors, for displaying favourite pieces of china or dinner-
ware. If there is space, a large cupboard that reaches to the

*Cupboards and drawers
come in a wide variety of
shapes and sizes which is
just what is needed to make
the most of storing the
contents of a kitchen.*

ceiling will provide splendid opportunities for storage.

Open plate racks or shelves are the perfect home for everyday china, and again add decorative detail to the room while supplying storage that is easily accessible. Position such storage racks within easy reach of the dishwasher or sink to save time and breakages.

For those who have moved into an older house in which there is a pantry, please think twice before having it removed. Unless the kitchen is extremely small, the traditional shelved, walk-in pantry can house far more than the best fitted kitchen layout. Originally, the pantry would have been situated on an outside wall with good ventilation and this – coupled with a stone floor – would have created a cool, airy space.

Today, despite central heating, pantries are still surprisingly efficient at keeping food and wine cool. In fact, many kitchen designers are now incorporating large floor to ceiling pantry or larder cupboards to replace the originals.

Modern designs of kitchen offer many storage solutions, such as fold-away ironing boards, pull-out rubbish bins and tables, and waste disposal units to keep the kitchen as streamlined as possible. Drawers of varying sizes are especially useful for storing different sized items. Small drawers are great for cutlery and tea-towels, say, while deep drawers make it easy to store larger items like casserole dishes and stacks of plates. Plan your requirements and then choose your units accordingly.

Saucepans and other kitchen utensils can be decorative so hang them up as a display and use the cupboards for other, less attractive, kitchenware.

If you have room to stow a large refrigerator elsewhere, you will find it useful to keep a small fridge in the kitchen for everyday items.

A mixture of storage in a contemporary, Shaker style. The peg board is set around the whole room and is perfect for hanging almost anything; the wicker drawers not only look good but also provide excellent storage for fruit and vegetables. And note the useful and decorative plate rack.

Unless totally bespoke, even the modern fitted kitchen will have the odd space where the smallest standard unit is too large to fit. Ask a carpenter to help you adapt these spaces to house thin baking tins or chopping boards, and consider replacing the plinth panels at the bottom of your kitchen base units with custom-made drawers to store linen or baking equipment. All too often it is these last pieces of equipment with their awkward shapes that clutter full-size cupboards.

If you have the advantage of a separate utility room, use it to house a large refrigerator or freezer, and fit a small integrated larder refrigerator, which will take up minimum space, in the kitchen. This can house the items that you most regularly use such as milk, butter and cheese, while larger items can be stored elsewhere until needed.

Be ruthless when it comes to organizing the contents of your kitchen. If something is used less than once a week it should not

These attractive wall units, designed in Art Deco style, provide storage with flair. Remember that wall units make good use of areas that would otherwise be wasted.

take up prime-access storage space. Conversely, condiments, herbs, spices and oils used regularly in cooking should be kept near to the cooker and easily accessible. Cooking pots and pans should be within easy reach, too, and can even add atmosphere to a room if displayed within view. This then frees up valuable cupboard space for other, less attractive, items, or items that are used less frequently.

The kitchen with good storage, then, has a mixture of built-in and open storage that has been carefully planned. This, combined with the good positioning of the contents of your kitchen, will offer you the best in storage solutions.

A well-planned kitchen has plenty of storage space. Mix glass-fronted cupboards with those that conceal appliances and unattractive cookware.

*Glazed or mirrored wardrobe
doors can be used to add
interest, or can help to
break up a long run of
matching furniture.*

The perfect solution to storage problems in the bedroom is to
have a dressing room, a separate area that is used specifically for
the storage of clothes. But few of us can afford to use an additional room just for this purpose, so we need to find other ways
around the problem. Clothes are normally the item that require
most consideration as the majority of garments are better hung
than stored flat, but note the proportion of items within your
wardrobe that require hanging space as this will give you a good
guide to your requirements. Bear in mind that less frequently used

*This hand-built fitted
cupboard has been
combined with additional
free-standing furniture to
create a traditional setting,
with ample storage for both
clothes and bed linen.*

Ever-changing children's rooms can benefit from free-standing smaller pieces as they can be rearranged at intervals to create a variety of layouts.

items, such as luggage, bed linen or sports equipment, can be stored elsewhere.

Once a decision has been made on the quantity and form of storage required, then you can consider the decorative style. Think of the finished look you wish to achieve in your bedroom before commiting yourself to the style of storage. Even colours should be looked at in detail. For traditional settings, painted or timber furniture is best, and although fitted furniture offers the best storage solutions, individual, free-standing pieces are the most successful in a cottage or Shaker-style setting. The modern home, however, can benefit from a wider range of styles. Easy-to-clean particle-board and melamine are very practical.

Furniture layout is also very important as it can affect the aesthetic proportions of the room. For example, avoid a run of units at one height down the longest wall of a narrow room as this will draw the eye along the wall, making it look even longer. The best option here is to change the height at intervals or stop the run of furniture and restart it further along the wall.

Look out for many of the specially designed features now included in fitted and free-standing furniture. They include linen baskets and shoe and tie racks.

An ingenious washbasin with built-in swivel drawers provides perfect storage for stocks of soaps and hand towels.

Storage requirements for bathrooms are not major, mainly consisting of space for towels, toiletries and cleaning materials and somewhere secure for medicines. It is also useful to have surface space beside basins, showers and baths for items in use, a towel rack for wet towels and a place for toys in a family bathroom.

Manufacturers offer various fixtures and fittings to maximize storage: a wall-hung basin, for example, allows space for cupboards underneath, which can be topped with a useful work surface. This has the added advantage of covering in the plumbing.

If you are creating a custom-built bathroom in an attic or

Fitted units around and above a wall-hung basin provide sleek, practical storage space.

Built-in shelves beside the bath provide useful storage for towels at the bottom as well as a display area for collectables on the less accessible upper shelves.

dormer room, you can make maximum use of available space by setting the bath, which doesn't require head room, under a sloping roof and building in shelves beside it. Shelves can also be fitted above a close-coupled toilet or the cistern can be fitted

The false wall to hide the cistern has been continued as a dado panel round the whole room to make a decorative feature.

A simple curtain, hung on a wire under the sink, makes an ideal tidy for ugly pipes or bathroom necessities.

behind a half-height false wall, finished off with a shelf. If you are having a built-in shower, make sure that it includes shelves for shampoos and soaps but keep these out of the line of the water.

If you are adapting an existing bathroom, a simple and inexpensive solution to providing covered storage is to fit a gathered curtain on a stretchable wire round the washbasin. This provides floor space for cleaning materials and keeps them out of sight. On the other hand, open shelves provide an opportunity to display attractive accessories or ornaments. Stacked towels, for instance, can brighten up a neutral coloured bathroom or accentuate a bright colour scheme.

Open shelving in a bathroom can be made into a decorative feature. These limed oak shelves complement the country style of the fittings.

The type of storage you choose for a bathroom will be defined by its style. A modern bathroom is more likely to have built-in, enclosed cupboards, so that the surfaces are uncluttered and the general appearance is smooth and sleek. Towel rails and other fixtures will be in chrome and glass. A period-style or country cottage bathroom will have free-standing units and wall-hung, open shelving. The emphasis will be on wood for all fixtures and fittings. This gives an opportunity to search out pieces of furniture from junk shops and have fun transforming them with one of the many decorative paint techniques, such as staining, stencilling or lime washing.

STOCKISTS

Alexander Beauchamp
Appleby Business Centre
Appleby Street
Blackburn
Lancashire BB1 3BL
Tel: 01254 691133
(Hand-printed wallpaper
and fabrics)

Amdega Conservatories
Faverdale Industrial
Estate
Darlington
Co Durham
DL3 0PW
Tel: 01325 468522

Appeal Blinds
6 Vale Lane
Bedminster
Bristol BS3 5SD
Tel: 0117 963 7734

C.P. Hart
213 Newnham Terrace
Hercules Road
London SE1 7DR
Tel: 020 7902 1000
(Bathrooms)

Caradon Bathrooms
Lawton Road
Alsager
Stoke-on-Trent ST7 2DE
Tel: 01270 879777

Colefax & Fowler
118 Garratt Lane
Wandsworth
London SW18 4DJ
Tel: 020 8874 6484
(Interiors and fabrics -
phone for other
branches)

Cope & Timmins Ltd
Head Office
Angel Road Works
Advent Way
Edmonton
London N18 3AY
Tel: 020 8803 6481
Branches in Birmingham,
Bristol and Leeds
(window furnishings)

Crown Paints
Tel: 01254 704951
(for stockists)

Crowson Fabrics
Headquarters
Crowson House
Bellbrook Park
Uckfield
East Sussex
TN22 1QZ
Tel: 01825 761055
(Made-to-measure
service)

Crucial Trading Ltd
Duke Place
Kidderminster
Worcestershire
Tel: 01562 825656
(Natural floor coverings)

Designers Guild
277 Kings Road
London
SW3 5EN
Tel: 020 7351 5775

Domicil
8850 Weingarten
Am Rebhang 2
Germany
Tel: 0751 48832
(Furniture)

Ducal
Northway
Andover
Hampshire
SP10 5AZ
Tel: 01264 333666
(Furniture)

Dulux Paints
Tel: 01753 550555
(customer services)

Fired Earth
Twyford Mill
Oxford Road
Adderbury
Oxon OX17 3SX
Tel: 01295 812088
(Tiles, flooring, fabrics)

**The General Trading
Company**
144 Sloane Street
London SW1X 9BL
Tel: 020 7730 0411

Graham & Greene
4 Elgin Crescent
London
W11 2HX
Tel: 020 7727 4594
and
164 Regents Park Road
London
NW1 8XN
Tel: 020 7586 2960

Habitat
Tel: 020 7255 2545
(Branches throughout
the UK - phone for your
nearest)

Heal's
196 Tottenham Court
Road
London W1T 7LG
Tel: 020 7636 1666

The Holding Company
Unit 2, Finchley Industrial
Centre
879 High Road
London
N12 8QA
Tel: 020 8445 2888
(Mail order storage)

The Iron Bed Company
Tel: 01243 578888
(Phone for mail order
brochure or nearest
showroom)

Laura Ashley
Tel: 0870 562 2116
(customer services)

MacCulloch & Wallis Ltd
25 Dering Street
London
W1S 1 AT
Tel: 020 7629 0311
(Fabrics with extensive
range of silks)

MFI
Head Office
Southon House
333 The Hyde
Edgware Road
London NW9 6TD
Tel: 0870 607 5093
(Phone for details of your
nearest store)

Mr Light
279 Kings Road
London SW3 5EW
Tel: 020 7352 8398
(Contemporary lighting)

Parador
Postfach 1741
48637 Coesfeld
Germany
Tel: 02541 7360
Fax: 02541 736213
(Storage)

Today Interiors
Hollis Road
Grantham
Lincs NG31 7QH
Tel: 01476 574401
(Furnishing fabrics and
wall coverings)

Poliform SpA
Via Magni 2
1-22044 Inverigo
Italy
Tel: 031 695111
Fax: 031 699444

Pots and Pithoi
The Barns
East Street
Turners Hill
West Sussex RH10 4QQ
Tel: 01342 714793
Fax: 01342 71700
(Plant pots)

Rolf Benz AG
Halterbacher Strasse
104
72202 Nagold
Germany
Tel: 07452 601-0
(Modern furniture)

Sanderson
233 Kings Road
London
SW3 5EJ
Tel: 020 7351 7728
(Fabrics)

Shaker
72 Marylebone High
Street
London
W1U 5JW
Tel: 020 7935 9461
(Furniture, gifts and
accessories. Mail order
available)

Sharps Bedrooms
Head Office
Albany Park
Camberley
Surrey
GU15 2PL
Tel: 01276 691534

Specialist Crafts Ltd
PO Box 38
Leicester
LE1 9BU
Tel: 0116 251 0405
Fax: 0116 251 5015
www.homecrafts.co.uk
(Mail order - large supply
of craft materials)

The Stencil Store
41 A Heronsgate Road
Chorleywood
Herts WD3 5BL
Tel: 01923 285577
Fax: 01923 285136

V V Rouleaux
6 Marylebone High
Street
London
W1U 4NP
Tel: 020 7224 5179
(Ribbons, trimmings and
braid)

SOUTH AFRICA

Biggie Best
Head Office
1 Fir Street
Observatory
Cape Town
Tel: (021) 448 1264
Fax: (021) 448 7057
(Branches countrywide)

Boardmans
Head Office/Warehouse
36 Auckland Street
Paarden Eiland
Cape Town
Tel: (021) 510 4700
Fax: (021) 510 3125
(Branches throughout.
Bedding, blinds, lamps,
bedside tables,etc.)

Wardkiss Homecare
Blue Route Centre
Tokai
Cape Town
Tel: (012) 72 5000
and
329 Sydney Road
Durban
Tel: (031) 25 1551
and
38 East Bruger Street
Bloemfontin
Tel: (051) 30 1888
(General hardware)

AUSTRALIA

BBC Hardware
Branches throughout
Australia
Contact Head Office
Building A, Cnr
Cambridge & Chester
Streets
Epping
NSW 2121
Tel: 02 9876 0888

Mitre 10
Branches nationwide,
contact:
319 George Street
Sydney
NSW 2000
Tel: 02 9262 1435
Customer service:
13 6310
www.mitre10.com.au

True Value Hardware
For branches, contact:
1367 Main North Road
Para Hills West
SA 5096
Tel: 08 8285 0600
or
16 Cambridge Street
Rocklea
QLD 4106
Tel: 07 3892 0892

Makit Hardware
35 branches, contact:
11-15 MacKay Street
Kewdale
WA 6105
Tel: 08 9352 4777

NEW ZEALAND

Carpet Court
57 Barrys Point Road
Takapuna
Tel: 09 489 9094

Levene & Co Ltd
Head Office
Harris Road
East Tamaki
Tel: 09 274 4211

Mitre 10
Head Office:
182 Wairau Rd
Glenfield
Auckland
Tel: 09 443 9900

Placemakers
Support Office
150 Marua Road
Panmure
Auckland
Tel: 09 525 5100

Resene Colour Shops
Tel: 04 577 0500
www.resene.co.nz

This edition published in 2003 by
New Holland Publishers (UK) Ltd
Garfield House, 86-88 Edgware Road, London W2 2EA, United Kingdom
www.newhollandpublishers.com
London • Cape Town • Sydney • Auckland

2 4 6 8 10 9 7 5 3

ISBN 1 85974 036 7

Designed by: Grahame Dudley Associates
Special Photography: Janine Hosegood
Editor: Louisa Somerville
Managing Editor: Coral Walker

Reproduction by Modern Age Repro House Ltd, Hong Kong
Printed and bound in Malaysia by Times Offset (M) Sdn Bhd

Acknowledgements

The authors and publishers would like to
thank the following companies and their PR
agencies for their kind assistance in the loan
of photographs and props used in this book.
We have taken care to ensure that we have
acknowledged everyone and we apologise if,
in error, we have omitted anyone.

For use of props/transparencies:
Alno Kitchens: 114-115
Amdega Conservatories: 117b
Appeal Blinds: 116
Andrew Macintosh Furniture: 48b, 178, 179t
Artisan: 77t, 83t
Azko Nobel: 149b
Bisque Radiators: 146b
C P Hart: 42t, 46, 47, 56t and b, 57, 124,
126, 127, 143, 184t
Caradon Bathrooms: 44, 59b, 78b, 86t, 148,
153t
Chadder: 42b
Colorol: 61b, 92b
Cope & Timmins Ltd: 29t, 131t
Crown Paints: 149b
Crucial Trading: 54t, 118
Daryl 43, 113t, 184b, 186b
Dorma: 69b
Dulux: p9, 18, 21, 25, 55, 61t, 90, 94, 101,
104b, 105, 106, 110t, 133
Fired Earth: 10t, 59t, 88, 135b, 147b, 151t
and b

Forbes & Lomax: 172t
Chloe Gardner: 16b
Gaston Y Daniela: 95b
Habitat: 54b, 82, 87t, 100b
Ideal Standard: 16, 45, 78t, 87, 89, 146t,
152t and b, 185, 186t
The Holding Company: 103b, 183t
The Iron Bed Company: 163
Laura Ashley: 47, 77, 83
Linens Select 86b
Matki Plc 112, 122
MFI: 102, 168, 181, 182t
Mr Light: 60
Heather Luke: 38, 157b
Nimbus: 27tr
Nolte Kitchens: 180
Parador: 173, 176
Pippa & Hale: 161t
Poliofrom 177b
Pret a Vivre: 47t, 100t
Qualitas 10b, 58, 79, 113b, 123, 149t, 153b, 187
Rolf Benz: 117t, 162, 164
Sanderson Collection: 23
Shaker: 95t
Sharps Bedrooms: 183b
Smallbone of Devizes: 79b, 81
Suzanne Malyon Designs: 135t
The Naked Zebra: 62t
The Stencil Store: 110b
Teuco 125
Viners of Sheffield plc: 36t
Wellmann Contessa: 48t
William Ball: 11
Wilman Fabrics and Wallpapers: 38b

Picture Credits:

Abode: half title, 27tl, 40-41, 51, 68, 73t,
75b, 129t, 150, 152, 156, 157t, 180t
Elizabeth Whiting Associates: Contents tr,
29b, 33, 34, 37, 60t, 75t, 108, 109, 119,
128b, 137, 166t, 169b
Picture Perfect: 145b, 174
Rupert Horrox: 24, 144
Interior Archive: 99; (Ari Ashley) 169t;
(Tim Beddow) 39, 74, 182b; (Simon Brown)
52; (Schulenburg) 17, 71t, 76, 96, 147t, 167,
175t; (Henry Wilson) 63
Julian Cotton Photo Library: 69t
Lizzie Orme: 12-13
Mainstream: Contents br, 6-7, 13t, 49t and
b, 62b, 93, 111t and b, 134, 165t and b,
166b, 170, 175b
Paul Ryan/International Interiors: 67, 139,
155, 161b; (John Fell Clark) title; (Frances
Halliday) 27bl; (Jo Nahem) 27br; (Rex
Jackson) 130
Philip Ennis Photography: (designer -
Bennet Weinstock) 31; (designer - Richard
Schlisinger Interior Design) 145t;
(designer - SGH Designs/Stephen & Gail
Huberman) 177t
Zefa: 26

INDEX

All entries in *italics* represent photographs

A
accent colours, 22-5, *23*, 55, 64, 76, 96, 98-9, 101, 107, 118, 133, 141, 155
accessories:
  bathroom, 42, 45, 59, *59*, 78, 86, *87*, 113, *113*
  bedroom, 39, 77, 92, 95
  bedsit, 135
  hallway, 131, 132, *132*, 133
  kitchen, 50, *50, 51*, 72, *72, 73*, 115, *115*
  living room, 66, 71, 96

B
bath, roll-top 42, 44, 47
bathroom:
  layout, 9
  lights, 175
  storage, 113, 184-7
bathrooms, 42-7, 56-9, 78-9, 86-9, 112-113, 146, 148-9, 152-3, 184-7
beams, 75, *75*, 82, *83*
bed linen, 40, 69, *69*, 110, 162, 163
bedding, 62
bedroom:
  colour schemes, 17
  contemporary, 61, *61*
  layout, 9
  lighting, 171
bedrooms: 22-3, 38-41, 60-3, 68-9, 90-5, 106-111, 158-9, 168, 182
beds, 76, 90, 92, *137*
bedsits, 134-141
bedspread, 163
bedsteads, 60, *60*
blinds:
  conservatory, 116, 121
  roller, 64, 154, 156
  Roman, 93, *93*, 100, 152, 153, *153*, 156
  Venetian, 152, *152*, 154, 157
  tie-up, 153
blockwork, *130*, 131
borders, decorative 35, 103
boxes, 95
boxing in, 47

C
canopy, 164, 168
carpets, 54, 55, 86, 141, 144, 145, *145*, 146, *146*
ceilings, 20, 30, 66, 70, 92,

104, 108, 134
chairs, 36, *38*, 38, 80, *80*, 133
chandeliers, 173
children's rooms, 102-115
cloakrooms, 122-127, *123*
coffee tables, 98
coir matting, 54, *54*
colours:
  bold, 66-7
  contrasting, 14, 37, 22-5
  cool, 15, 24, 50, 53, 79, 88, 90, 100, 118
  dark, 18, 20
  harmonious, 14
  historical, 35, 36, 42, 44
  monochromatic, 49, 46, 96, 98, 136, 141, 163
  natural, 131
  neutral, 61, 86, 92, 98, 130, 139, 163
  pale, 20
  pastel, 53, 58, 59, 108-9, 119
  power of, 16-17
  primary, 14, 15
  secondary, 14, 15
  tertiary, 14, 15
  warm, 15, 119, 130
colour schemes, 12-25, 53
colour wheel, 14-15, *15*, 24, 53, 65, 104-5, 132, *159*
conservatory:
  insulation, 116
  ventilation, 116
conservatories, 116-121
contemporary styles, 48-67
contrasts, 22-5
coronas, 107, *165*
cottage styles, 68-85
country styles, 68-85
cupboards, 141, 178, *178, 181, 182*, 184
curtain poles, 29, 47, *77*
curtains, 20, 38, 40, 41, *41*, 130, 133, 154-5, *155, 156*, 167
cushions, 71, *71, 157, 161*
cushion covers, 161, *161*
cutlery, 36, 37

D
dado rail, 28, *42*, 43, 59, 106, *106*, 107, 145, 149
decoupage, 30, *46*, 47, 102
dimmer switches, 36
dining rooms, 36-7, *37*, 171, 173, 54-5, 118-9
distemper, 74, 97
drapes, 30-1, 64, *65*, 109, *109*, 111, 165-6, *179*

drawing rooms, 64
dressers, 84-5
dressing rooms, 182

E
electrical points, 35

F
fabric:
  chintz, 70
  check, 73, *73*
  gingham, 100
    fabrics, 40, 66, 76, 77, 95, 158-169
  sheer, 153
flooring:
  coir, 146
  cushioned, 82
  flagstone, 82
  linoneum, 100
  matting, 132, 145
  natural, 145, *146*
  pine, 64
  stained, 78, *79*
  terracotta, *42*, 43, 151
  tiled, 70, *88*, 113, 146, *151*
  timber, 28, 50, 51, *51*, 59, 91, 135, 136, 139, 146, 147, 151
  vinyl, 47, 151
floors, 20, 69, 144-151
four-poster beds, 163, *163*, 164, *167*
frieze, 58, *59*
furniture:
  conservatory, 117, *117*
  distressed, 92, *92*
  fitted, 103, *183*
  free-standing, *183*
  hall, 133
  semi-industrial, 136
  traditional, 139
  upholstered, 97

G
garden rooms, 116-121
graphite, 136

H
hallways, 20, *24*, 128-133
half-tester, 109, 164
hob, 114

I
intaglio designs, 148
J
jute and cotton, 124, 130

K
kelim rugs, 35

kitchen units:
  island, 53, *53*
  oak, 34, *34*
  painted, 81, *81*
kitchen:
  contemporary, 48
  cottage, 74-5, *75*
  country, 80-1
  fitted, 114, *115*
  galley, *11*
  layout, 10
  lighting, 170
  painted, 32, 33, *33*, 84, *84*
  pine, 72-3, 82-3, *83*
  planning, 52
kitchen designers, 10
kitchen ranges, 32, 72, 83, *147*
kitchens, 50-3, 72-5, 80-85,
    100-1, 114-5, 147, 151,
    156-7, 167, 178, 180,
kitchenware, 101

L
lamp shades, 174
lamps, 31, 40-1, *41*
layout and planning, 8-11
light:
  evening, 17, 120
  morning, 17
  natural, 52, 128
light and shade, 120-1
light switches, 171, 172, *172*
lighting, 31, 40-1, 56, 67, 99,
    116, 127, 129, 170-175
lights:
  fluorescent, 170
  halogen, *17*, 56, 170, *171*,
    173
  pelmet, 174
  pendant, 36
  recess, 170, 172
  side, 171, 175
  spot, 170, 171, 172, 175
  strip, 175
  tungsten, 141
liming, 64, 69, 74
living rooms, 31-2, 70-1, 96-9,
    154, 160, 166, 176
loft rooms, 136-7

M
masonry sealant, 149
mirrors, 135, *135*, 138, *138*
Moroccan style, 134-5
motifs, 107
murals, 102, *102*, 169, *169*

N
natural dyes, 62
nurseries, 25

O
ovens, 114

P
paints, 32, 35, 46, 54, 69, 89,
    148, 147, 150
pantries, 179
pattern, 30-31
pelmets, 28
pictures, 28-9, 41, 62, 63,
    71, 93, 105, *105*, 107,
    128
planning permission, 121
planning the layout, 8-11
plants, 49, 55, 65, 66, 99,
    120, 121, *121*, 139
plumbing, 10

Q
quilt covers, 107

R
room proportions, 20, 28
rugs, *31*, 70, 78, *79*, 88, 91

S
scale drawings, 9
Shaker style, 94-5, *94*
shelving, 70, *70*, 78, *78*, 125,
    138, 176, 177, *177*, 179,
    185, 186, 187
showers, 122-127
shutters, *90*, 91, 154, 157
sitting rooms, 20
smocking, 108
sofas, 8, 160, *160, 162, 164*,
    166
soft furnishings, 91, 135,
    158-169
sponging 123
staircases, *130*, 131
steel, 136
stencilling, 69, 86, 150
storage:
  bathroom, 184-187
  bedroom, 90, 103, *103*, 111
bedsits, 138, 140
storage solutions, 176-189
studio rooms, 134-141

T
tiebacks, 108

tiles:
  ceramic, 32, *32, 42*, 43, *59*,
    88, 146, *146*, 147, *147*,
    148, 150, 151, *151*,
  cork, 47, 151
  handmade, 135
  Moroccan-style, 135
  pressed, 81, *81*
toile de Jouy, 39
tone, 18-21, 53, 55, 61, 67,
    98, 101, 136-7
tones:
  contrasting, 39
  neutral, 38, 88
traditional styles, 28-47
tranquil styles, 86-101
tribal design, 62, *63*
trompe l'oeil, 42, *42*

U
upholstery, 31, 161
utility rooms, 180

W
wall coverings, 42, 145, 146,
    147, 148, 149
wallpaper, 33, 108,
walls, 36, 69, 97, 106, 121,
    131, 134, 144-151
wardrobes, fitted, 9, *68, 182*,
    182
wash basins, 9, *42*
window treatments, 34, 45, *45*,
    98, 104, 152-157, 166
windows:
  arched, 130
  casement 64, 65
  French, 117, *117*
wrought iron, 74, 76, 77, 92